Books by Allan W. Eckert

BLUE JACKET

BLUE JACKET

War Chief of the Shawnees

ALLAN W. ECKERT

LITTLE, BROWN AND COMPANY

Boston   Toronto

LIBRARY OF CONGRESS CATALOG CARD NO. 69-10656

01283   W0251

Ninth Printing

BP

*Published simultaneously in Canada
by Little, Brown & Company (Canada) Limited*

PRINTED IN THE UNITED STATES OF AMERICA

For

Nelson Valjean

. . . a good friend who has always
been distant in miles, but very
close in spirit . . .

Author's Note

Blue Jacket, the famous Shawnee War Chief who was also known as Marmaduke Van Swearingen and Weh-yah-pih-ehr-sehn-wah, was a real person and this is the story of his life — the story of a young white settler on the frontier who longed to be an Indian and actually became one.

Much of Blue Jacket's life is documented but there are certain gaps in the story. In this book, the author has taken the liberty of smoothing these gaps and building a complete story. This was done only after a careful study of all the known facts of Blue Jacket's life. All of the major incidents described in the book are true; the author has taken license only with minor items which do not affect or alter history. Much of the dialogue is taken directly from historical records, but a certain amount was created to help maintain the smooth flow characteristic of a novel.

The Ohio Country referred to in the book includes all of the present state of Ohio and parts of eastern Indiana and southern Michigan. The Northwest Territory referred to includes Ohio, Indiana, Illinois, Michigan and Wisconsin — largely the original Northwest Territory.

Descriptions of Shawnee customs and language come from historical records, and the dances, games, sports, social life and other aspects of Shawnee life are closely documented.

All of the other characters in this book, both Indian and white, were real people who lived the life and did the things they are depicted as having lived and done. No fictional characters will be found in this book.

LAKE ERIE

SWAN CREEK

JOSEPH'S RIVER

MAUMEE RIVER

FORT DEFIANCE

AUGLAZE R.

ST. MARYS R.

WABASH R.

GIRTY'S TOWN

INDIAN LAKE

BLUE JACKET'S TOWN

MACKACHACK

FORT GREENVILLE

FORT JEFFERSON

PIQUA TOWN

CHILLICOTHE
(BLACK FISH'S VILLAGE)

MIAMI RIVER

SCIOTO RIVER

KISPOKO TOWN

HOCKHOCKING R.

LOGAN'S VILLAGE

CRESAP'S CAMP

MARIETTA

OHIO RIVER

FORT HAMILTON

LITTLE MIAMI R.

FORT WASHINGTON

LICKING RIVER

LIMESTONE CREEK
THREE ISLANDS

CABIN CREEK

MAYSVILLE
LIMESTONE AREA

BLUE LICKS

McCLELLAND'S STATION

POINT PLEASANT

FORDING PLACE

GREAT KANAWHA R.

N

BLUE JACKET'S COUNTRY

MAP BY LORENCE BJORKLUND

BLUE JACKET

I

Wednesday Morning, June 5, 1771

"Listen, Marmee, you dunderhead," Vance said irritably, "it's about time you quit playing like as if you was a stupid Injen. There jest ain't no good reason for you all the time running off into the woods and hunting with that crazy bow and arrow. What for you think Paw give you that gun?"

Vance Van Swearingen paused to give his younger brother a chance to reply, but when the boy merely stared at him and tightened his lips, he shook his head. "Sometimes nowadays," he said, "I get to thinking maybe Tom's right and you are sort of funny in the head. Ain't normal for nobody to like Injens like you do and try to act like 'em all the time. 'Bout time you start acting like a white boy, hear?"

The boy he had called Marmee still said nothing and merely continued lacing a high moccasin around his calf. Vance snorted. "Dang Injen-lover. You like savages so much, whyn't you jest go on and live with 'em 'stead of hanging around here. Ain't none of us wants to have no dang Injen-lover in the fam'ly. Reckon you need to be straightened out some."

Vance turned on his heel and strode from the room, banging the door loudly after him. For a long while the younger boy remained motionless, lost in thought. He hadn't trusted himself to answer when Vance was talking because it would have ended up in another fight. Not that he couldn't take Vance, if it came to that; Vance might be six years older, but he wasn't fast enough any more, or strong enough or even big enough. But if they *had* fought, his other brothers would have come running and long ago he had learned he couldn't fight all of them at once.

The boy grunted in anger and frustration. He began to wind the long rawhide laces of his moccasin boot around his other leg. Why, he wondered, couldn't his family understand how he felt? After all, whether they liked it or not, Indians were people, not animals.

The cabin door banged open again and his younger brother, twelve-year-old Charley, clattered in. His sand-colored hair was mussed and his eyes were flashing with excitement.

"Whooo-eee! You sure got Vance all stirred up, Duke. He's out there telling the others that you're aiming to go out and act like a savage again. Telling 'em they all oughta get you out there and teach you another lesson."

His eyes widened and he added hastily, "I think they really aim to do it, too, Duke. Better light out in a hurry or you're in for it. And this time Paw ain't home to bust it up."

The older boy nodded. It wouldn't be the first time he had been ganged up on by his elder brothers — John, Tom, Steel, Vance and Joe. Moving quickly, he finished lacing his moccasin and then from the table scooped up his narrow-bladed skinning knife in its bark sheath and shoved it into the waistband of his coarsely woven trousers. It was not the first time his younger brother had warned him in time and he was grateful to Charley. Grateful, too, that Charley continued to call him Duke rather than that detestable nickname of Marmee which all the rest of them used.

His name was Marmaduke Van Swearingen and he was seventeen years old. Tall for his age, he was well built, his hair very dark and his features well formed. And, much to the disgust of nearly everyone who knew him, he had an abiding admiration for Indians. It didn't matter what tribe they belonged to, either; Duke simply felt that the Indians had been very badly treated by whites in almost every encounter and that their way of life was better by far than the white man's ways.

The fact that outlying settlements and isolated cabins nearby had been attacked on occasion and their occupants killed by marauding Indians made little difference to him.* After all, the whites *had* stolen their

* The Van Swearingen cabin was located near the present city of Richwood, West Virginia.

lands, hadn't they? And how many Indians had been killed by the whites without just cause? As far as Duke was concerned, the Indians had good reason for their raids.

Now, from a peg near the door he took down a light-blue hunting shirt woven of flax and wool — the material commonly called linsey-woolsey — and put it on over his bare and well-tanned chest. It really looked more like a vest now than the carefully constructed long-sleeved garment his mother had made for him. The collar was gone, he had ripped off both sleeves to the shoulders and only one button remained to hold it together.

He strode over to his low bed, hardly more than a pallet on the floor, and took down from the wall a highly polished bow and raccoon-skin quiver. The eight or nine arrows in the quiver were fletched with turkey feathers and tipped with sharpened pieces of bone.

Alongside where the bow had hung was an old but serviceable musket, a birthday present his father had given him last March. Duke suspected it was just one more effort by his parent to rid him of the strong admiration he felt for the red man and his ways.

Ever since he was nine he had wanted to be like them. When he heard of encounters between white men and Indians he always, with a perverse loyalty, felt a lift of his spirits if it had been the whites who were bested. More than once he had announced wistfully that when he became a man he would take up the wonderfully free life of the Indians and live his days out happily with some tribe.

At first his parents, brothers and sister had just

nodded and grinned, considering it a passing fancy; but it hadn't passed and now it was an issue which continued to irk the entire family. They felt Duke was the laughingstock of all their neighbors and that it was shameful of him to embarrass them in such manner. Their father had echoed the sentiments of the family when he said:

"Marmee, don't talk so foolish. Indians ain't to be fooled with and they ain't to be admired nohow. And far as you joining up with 'em, I reckon you ever *did* see one a-coming at you, you'd hightail it home like they was a devil licking at your heels."

The family's disbelief and attempts at discouragement had not dampened his conviction, but he talked less about it as time passed. Nevertheless, he still took constant jibes from them because he preferred the bow for hunting over his musket and because he liked to dress himself Indian fashion.

Charley was peeking through a crack in the door as Duke finished his preparations but now he whirled around and whispered urgently, "They're coming, Duke, all five of 'em."

Duke nodded. "I'll skin out the back window," he said. "See you later, Charley."

As he began to open the small window, Charley ran to his side. "Help me up, Duke. I'm going with you." He continued hastily when Duke started to shake his head, "Don't tell me no! I warned you, didn't I? And you know I don't care if you like Injens. I want to go hunting with you, Duke, *please!*"

"Paw'll tan you when we get home," Duke warned.

"I been tanned before. Once more won't kill me."

There wasn't time to argue. Duke could hear them coming now and so without another word he wrapped his arms about his little brother's middle and shoved the boy's legs through first, then lowered him to the ground. Next he handed out his bow and quiver.

"Marmee!" His oldest brother, John, was calling. "*Marmee!* Get out here and face what you got coming. We ain't gonna stand for no Injen-lover as a brother. Come on out right now!"

Duke grinned and hoisted himself up and out of the window headfirst, doing a smooth somersault as he touched the ground and immediately regaining his feet. In front, John was calling him again.

"Listen, Marmee, we don't want to mess up the house but either you come out by the time I count ten or we're gonna come in and drag you out, hear?"

Snatching up his weapons in one hand and grabbing Charley's small hand with the other, Duke ran toward the woods fifty yards away. Once there, he'd be safe. He knew more about cover, hiding and backtracking than the whole lot of them put together. But the trick was to get to that cover unseen. With Charley along he wouldn't be able to travel as rapidly or quietly. The brothers would not be apt to pursue unless they glimpsed them running. Even as they ran the voice of John came to them faintly.

". . . six . . . seven . . . eight . . ."

The pair plunged into the screen of woodland, and the cabin was almost immediately lost from sight and hearing. They did not hear John finish his count or see the rush of the five boys to the cabin door. Nor did they see the exasperation of the five when they discovered that there was no one inside.

They could imagine the reaction, however, and both of them laughed aloud as they followed a ravine toward a distant creek where Duke had often gone hunting.

II

Marmaduke Van Swearingen pulled off an excellent shot at the cottontail rabbit he and Charley had flushed from a patch of briers beside the creek.

The little animal sprang up from alongside a rotted log and raced in a zigzagging manner along the high bank for perhaps twenty yards before turning sharply to the right to enter the woods. Duke's bow twanged and, only an instant before the rabbit would have vanished, the arrow plunged through its hindquarters, impaling it to an emergent root of a huge old sycamore tree.

Charley whooped excitedly at his brother's shot and ran up to kill the animal, lopping off its head with his own broad-bladed hunting knife. He began skinning it and grinned up at his brother.

"Gosh, Duke, you're a sight better shot with a bow than most people with a gun."

Pleased at this praise and no little proud of his shot, Duke smiled. He wished his older brothers and father had seen it. Might make them realize his bow was not, as they put it, a toy. Charley, he was sure, would tell them all about it, but it wouldn't be the same as if they had seen it themselves.

They would have been very surprised, in fact, had they known the full extent of Duke's woods lore and knowledge of Indian ways. He had learned most of it from the old trapper and trader called Jacob by most of the people hereabouts. Duke knew him better as Chaqui — a shortening of the Algonquian word *chaquiweshe,* meaning mink, by which he had been known to the Shawnees.

One of the happiest days in the young life of Marmaduke Van Swearingen had come four years ago when the crippled old man had come to this area to settle down after many years of trading and living with the Indians. He had built a disreputable one-room cabin on this very creek, a few miles upstream from here and not very far from the Van Swearingen household.

Duke had quickly formed a strong liking for the man which bordered on hero worship. Jacob — or Chaqui — in turn felt a close attraction to the youth who reminded him so much of himself in his younger days. The boy spent much of his free time after that in Chaqui's cabin, helping him with many of the chores he was too crippled with arthritis to do well for himself, listening enthralled to the old man's never ending tales of his wilderness experiences, and learning survival in the wilds.

Duke always had many questions to ask about the Indians and Chaqui gave him the answers to the best of his knowledge. The boy even picked up a sizable vocabulary of Indian words which he practiced diligently. He could, he felt, make himself understood by an Indian if the opportunity ever came. It was a skill which no one but himself and the old man knew he possessed.

Even the bow that he had used in downing the rabbit had been fashioned of springy osage wood by Duke under the careful guidance of Chaqui, and it was indeed a fine weapon. They had also worked together in making the arrows of prime white cedar.

Since he was next to youngest in the family, Duke had often received rough treatment at the hands of his older brothers. But in the past few years, happily, they had not mauled him physically so much as they had when he was younger. In his fourteenth year he had begun to develop rapidly and now, at seventeen, he was unusually muscular, just under six feet tall and more active athletically than any of his brothers.

The older boys ridiculed Duke for spending so much time with Chaqui and even Duke's parents chided him constantly for his interest in Indians and in "that worthless old man." Of the whole family, only his older sister Sarah and little Charley sympathized to some extent.

Now, squatting to watch Charley as the boy continued with his cleaning of the rabbit, Marmaduke Van Swearingen looked very much like an Indian. His black hair was long and his handsome features somewhat angular. His cheekbones were high and the only thing which marred the smooth tan of his face was a small white scar like an inverted letter V over his right eyebrow; a scar put there two years before by Charley when he threw a sharp rock at a squirrel and accidentally hit Duke instead.

The tan of Duke's face was duplicated on his bare arms and on the wide expanse of bare chest which showed through the blue shirt held together only by that single button at his waist. On his feet he wore almost knee-high moccasins of soft buffalo hide. These had been given to him by Chaqui for his last birthday, along with the fine bone-handled knife now in his belt. The moccasins were high to protect against the strike of copperheads and timber rattlesnakes, which were common in this area. Faded coarse gray trousers completed his costume. Squatting in this way, with his bow in hand and quiver slung across his back, he could very easily have been mistaken for an Indian.

It was just as Charley was finishing that the boys heard a slight noise and looked up to find themselves in the center of a ring of eleven Shawnee warriors, some with tomahawks in their hands. Charley went pale and dropped his knife, but Duke reached out and touched his arm.

"Easy," he whispered. "They ain't painted, so that means they're not a war party. Prob'ly a hunting party. Sit still."

Moving slowly himself, Duke got to his feet and tossed his bow and quiver to the ground. The leader of the group was a squat, unsmiling individual wearing only

buckskin leggins and ankle-high moccasins. Duke nodded
to him but got no response.

"*Manese*," the youth said, a forced smile on his face,
remembering the word Chaqui had told him meant
knife. With his left hand, using only thumb and fore-
finger, he pulled the weapon from his belt and dropped
it to the ground beside the bow. Then he put out his
hand, palm upward, toward the leader of the party. The
Indian was holding a cocked flintlock rifle in his right
hand. It was pointed vaguely in the direction of the
boys.

"*Ne-kah-noh*," Duke said pleasantly, while Charley
watched and listened in amazement. "*Was-he-sheke*."

Duke almost laughed aloud, not only at Charley's
reaction, but at thinking how he himself might have felt
had he come across an Indian who threw down his
weapons and said in broken English, "Friend. Nice day."
But he noticed with satisfaction a general relaxing on the
parts of some of the hunters and was relieved to see the
leader gently lower the hammer of the firearm.

He pointed to Charley, who still was crouched more
or less frozen with fear, and added, *Ni jai-nai-nah. Mat-
tah tsi.*" — My brother. No kill.

The chief of the party nodded once and his face
remained expressionless as he spoke. One of his large
upper front teeth was very dark in color, as though
stained or decayed. While his words were delivered
more rapidly than Duke was accustomed to hearing from
Chaqui, the youth listened carefully and managed to get
the gist of what the Shawnee said. Choosing his own
words carefully and often hesitating as he sought to

recall the word or phrase he needed, he replied at length.

Then, for almost an hour, they talked. Now and then one of the other Indians commented, but mostly they just listened. It was an obviously difficult conversation for both parties, accompanied by many hand movements to put across proper meaning. At last, however, Duke showed his even white teeth in a broad grin. He turned and picked up both knives, the bow and quiver and handed them to the leader. Then he turned to Charley and spoke earnestly.

"Charley, listen carefully. They're Kispokothas — warrior Shawnees. The one I've been talking to is a subchief. His name is P'catewah Ki-be-tar-leh, which means Black Tooth. I got him to promise to let you go home unharmed if I go with them. They say they want to adopt me into their tribe."

He held up a hand as the boy, his eyes filling up with tears and chin beginning to tremble, started to protest. "No, Charley, listen to me; I'm going. It's what I've always dreamed of and it's the only way. I'm a little scared, but I think I'll be all right. But it's the only way. If I refuse to go with them now, they'll have to kill both of us.

"You go on home. Tell Maw and Paw and the others what happened, but tell 'em not to follow us or they might kill me. Or *they* might get killed. Remember that now, *they aren't to follow!* It'd only cause trouble."

A long tear dribbled down Charley's right cheek and he brushed it away with the back of his hand. Duke reached out and squeezed his shoulder, then helped him to his feet and hugged him tightly. Charley clung to him fiercely and his tears came in earnest then. After a moment, Duke gently pushed him away and held him at arm's length.

"Don't worry, Charley, they aren't going to hurt me, honest. They watched me shoot the rabbit and saw how I'm dressed and all. They're pleased that I want to be like them and they just want to adopt me. They've even given me a name already. Now go!"

He thrust his brother from him and Charley ran a dozen steps or so before abruptly stopping and looking back.

"What name, Duke?"

"Weh-yah-pih-ehr-sehn-wah."

Charley frowned. "What's that mean?"

Marmaduke Van Swearingen laughed and tapped the breast of his shirt with a finger. "Blue Jacket."

III

← ⎯⎯⎯⎯⎯⎯⎯⎯⎯⎯⎯⎯⎯⎯ ◄

Sunday, June 16, 1771

► ⎯⎯⎯⎯⎯⎯⎯⎯⎯⎯⎯⎯⎯⎯ →

Their reception at Kispoko Town, which was also known as Pucksinwah's Town, had a profound effect on Marmaduke Van Swearingen, although it was not exactly what he had expected it to be.

From what Chaqui had told him of the customs of the Shawnees and other Indian tribes, he knew that he would be required to run a gauntlet line when he reached the village. It was customary. He was not, however, prepared for it to be much of an ordeal.

The hunting party, after the departure of little Charley, had set off at once for the Ohio country where this village was located. Although at first they were careful about not leaving footprints or other sign of their passage, they made no effort to travel at great speed.

They moved along at an easy pace in a northwest-wardly direction and crossed the Elk River near the mouth of Sandy Creek.* Continuing in the same general direction, they encountered the Great Kanawha River and crossed it at a ford some twenty miles above its mouth,† and then followed it downstream to where it emptied into the Ohio River, which they called *Spay-lay-wi-theepi.*

The larger river was a quarter-mile or more wide at this point and here they stopped for a brief rest and discussion. Black Tooth instructed two of the hunters, who may have been brothers, to leave the main party and the pair set off at once. They shoved an old section of dried tree trunk into the Ohio and, clinging to it on opposite sides, kicked their way across. They came ashore far downstream, waved, then struck off diago-nally northwest along a trail through the hilly woods which led directly to Kispoko Town. The remainder of the party, including Duke, began following the south shore of the big river downstream.

There were two reasons for doing this. The first was so that the pair who crossed over could reach the village first with the news that a white youth was being brought in for possible adoption. The second reason was because the party had originally come down the Scioto River of the Ohio country in canoes. They had hidden them opposite that river's mouth on the south shore of the

---

* In the area of present Clendenin, West Virginia.

† This fording place, no longer apparent because of dams on the Kanawha River, was near the site of the present city of Leon, West Virginia.

Ohio. From there the hunting party had gone overland to the south and east in a great semicircle which had brought them to where Duke and Charley had been hunting.

On the fifth day after leaving the Kanawha, they reached the spot where the canoes had been hidden in a small, protected cove. The boats, three of them, had been weighted with rocks and sunk in about five feet of water. It took only a short while to find them, empty out the rocks and float them again in good condition.

At once they had crossed the Ohio and begun ascending the Scioto, largest river of the Ohio country. The journey upriver had taken two days and they stopped a mile short of Kispoko Town to let Duke and four of the Shawnees, including Black Tooth, alight on the shore to wait there for further word to advance. The three canoes then continued upstream.

Within an hour a troop of more than a dozen nearly naked boys Duke's age or younger whooped into sight astride horses and galloped madly around the four Indians and their captive for a few minutes before heading back to the village. This, Black Tooth told Duke, was the signal that the gauntlet lines had been formed and they were to come in.

That was when the shock came for Duke. Expecting perhaps twenty or thirty people to be lined up waiting, he experienced a sudden fear when he saw the assemblage. A double line of Indians stretched toward him a full quarter-mile from the *msi-kah-mi-qui* — the central council house.

The size of that building itself was a big surprise. Its

walls were built of evenly cut saplings, each about two inches in diameter and eight or nine feet high. The structure was about thirty feet wide and easily ninety feet long, with one large door in the center. It was to this door that the double line of Indians stretched.

As for the people themselves, there were hundreds gathered here and strung out in the double gauntlet line — men, women, boys, girls and even toddlers barely able to stand by themselves. All had some type of whipping device in their hands; willow switches, rawhide strips, light pieces of wood, broomstick-sized staffs and lengths of blackberry bush bristling with thorns. These were not only the people of Kispoko Town, but also many from the two Shawnee villages across the Scioto River and slightly downstream — the towns of the great Shawnee Chief Cornstalk and his huge sister, Non-hel-e-ma. *

In these eleven days that he had spent with Black Tooth's hunting party, Duke had quickly improved his Shawnee speech. He soon decided that what he had learned from Chaqui had been little indeed. By this time, though, while he was still a long way from being fluent in the tongue, he could converse well enough to be understood without too much difficulty, and he could understand them even better.

When they reached the mouth of the double line of

* Kispoko Town (or Pucksinwah's Town) was about two or three miles downstream from present Circleville, Ohio, on the west bank of the Scioto River. About a mile or so downstream on the opposite side, separated from one another by Scippo Creek, were Cornstalk's Town and Non-hel-e-ma's Town.

Indians, Black Tooth ordered Duke to remove all his clothes, even his moccasins. Embarrassed, Duke obeyed, and then surprised himself by standing erect with his head high and his arms at his sides. He made no attempt to shield his nakedness, despite the jeers and taunts and insulting remarks which arose all down the line.

The squat Black Tooth, with a trace of a smile curling his lips, kicked the clothing aside. Wordlessly he accepted a rather short but heavy staff handed him by a small boy who immediately rejoined the line with his own limber switch.

The Shawnee spoke to Duke, rubbing the staff as he did so. "When I touch you with this, you are to run between the lines to the *msi-kah-mi-qui.* You will not be struck from the front. No one will strike you until you begin to pass, *unless* you stop running or turn around. If you do that, it will be a sign of cowardice and adoption will be denied."

Duke swallowed and nodded. There was only one alternative to adoption: death. He determined to neither stop nor turn. He intended running as he had never run before. Perhaps, with luck, he could reach the central council house and the sanctuary within before too many blows struck him. Inwardly, he was quaking; the line was so long and with people striking at him from both sides, how could he possibly make it?

Black Tooth ordered Duke to bend over, facing down the slot between the double line. The murmur of voices faded into an expectant hush. Then, from near the *msi-kah-mi-qui* came the dull boom of a drum.

Duke expected the "touch" of Black Tooth's staff to

be less than gentle, but he was not prepared for the tremendous blow across his buttocks which sent a wave of pain through him and caused him to sprawl face down in the dirt. Amid shrieks and laughter, a rain of switches began lashing his backside and he struggled to his feet and began a desperate run.

Blow after blow struck him, stinging, welting, cutting, ripping the skin of his back, rump and legs. The pain was beyond description and his vision swam, but still he ran. Several times he stumbled, caught himself and ran on. Stones gouged his bare feet.

While the blows had never been gentle, they became even stronger and the weapons heavier as he progressed down the line. At about the halfway mark he turned his ankle and sprawled again, a low moan escaping him. A dreadful *thunk* sounded every time a blow struck and an awful numbness crept through him. For a fraction of a second he thought he would just lie there and let death come to end his torment.

But then he was up again, scampering along on all fours for the first dozen feet until he regained his balance and once again forced himself into a run. Through a haze of pain he saw the great looming bulk of the *msi-kah-mi-qui* no more than fifty yards ahead.

For a wild, exultant moment he really believed he would make it; that he would dive through the open doorway and just lie there basking in the glory of not being struck. But it was a hasty judgment.

In another dozen steps, during which he was struck repeatedly, he was suddenly hit an awful blow across the neck and he fell as if he had been shot. He managed to get back to his hands and knees, but no farther. Dimly he was aware that his nose was bleeding badly and his back was afire with pain.

A swarm of Indians crowded around him, screeching and flailing their weapons. His arms collapsed and his face hit the dirt. A moment later he rolled onto his side and, with the blows continuing at an even greater rate, he felt unconsciousness closing over him.

And in that instant before he was gone, he thought bitterly, "I've failed."

IV

Friday, July 5, 1771

It was more than two weeks before Marmaduke Van Swearingen was able to walk again without the healing wounds on back, buttocks and legs cracking open to leave him gasping in pain. He had remained unconscious until the morning after the gauntlet run. Even then, because several of his wounds became infected, he verged on delirium for two days more.

The Shawnees had been surprised, but not because he had not completed the gauntlet run. Rather, they were deeply impressed that he had traveled it so far — much farther, in fact, than a number of full-grown men brought captive here had gone.

Though not much more than a boy, he was shown the respect afforded to a very brave man. Under the care of squaws now deeply concerned for his welfare, he re-covered rapidly. They bathed his wounds repeatedly and gently rubbed a greasy, foul-smelling concoction which conquered the infection and encouraged healing.

He was supremely happy. This was the day, at last, when he was to be officially adopted into the Shawnee tribe. He was to become a member of the Kispokotha sept of the tribe. Further, he was being adopted into the family of the chief himself, Pucksinwah.

As with many Indian tribes, the Shawnees were di-vided into clanlike segments called septs. There were five of these septs and each, though governed by itself, provided an important function to the tribe as a whole.

The Peckuwe sept, for instance, had charge of main-taining order or duty and looked after celebrations of matters pertaining to Shawnee religion. The Maykujay sept controlled matters pertaining to health, medicine and food. The two most powerful septs, having charge of all things political and all matters affecting the entire tribe, were the Thawegila and Chalahgawtha septs. From one of them the principal chief of the Shawnee nation had to come. The chiefs of all the other septs were under control of the principal chief in all tribal matters, but in matters affecting only their own septs, they were independent chiefs.

The final sept — the Kispokotha — was in charge of all circumstances of warfare. This included the prepara-tion of warriors and the providing of a war chief for the entire tribe. It was a proud sept.

The principal chief now was a Chalahgawtha named Hokolesqua — Cornstalk — whose village was nearby. He would be on hand today to witness the ceremonies and welcome Duke into the tribe. But it was the tribal war chief and chief of the Kispokotha sept — Pucksinwah — who would be in charge.

Duke quickly learned that Pucksinwah was not only deeply loved and respected, his word was absolute law. He was a tall, strong man, noted for his kindness and generosity among his own people and his deadly fierceness against enemies.

Pucksinwah's wife, Methotasa, had borne him six children, and it was generally believed in the tribe that the chief was a favorite of Moneto, the Supreme Being of All Things. His oldest son, Chiksika, even though only fifteen, was already becoming noted for his strength and intelligence. Pucksinwah's thirteen-year-old daughter, Tecumapese, was just now beginning to bloom into the most beautiful maiden among the Kispokothas, if not the entire tribe.

The second son of the chief had been born just three years ago last March. At the instant of his birth a tremendous comet had seared the skies; a rare and inspiring omen, signifying greatness to come in the future of this chubby child. His name was Tecumseh.

And, as if Tecumseh's birth under the sign of the comet was not alone proof that Pucksinwah was favored by Moneto, there could be no doubt of it since the last Hunger Moon — January — for that was when the chief's wife had given birth to triplet boys. It was an event never before recorded in Shawnee history.

These matters of interest in the tribe and sept were explained to Duke by Chiksika. They felt a natural

boyish attraction for each other and a curiosity in each
for the other's way of life. Duke told him about his own
boyhood and family.

The brow of the chief's son wrinkled as he listened.
He was not able to understand such a family life as
Duke's, where the members were at odds with one another, with little or no interfamily respect, courtesy or
love. He continued to ask Duke penetrating questions
until they were interrupted. It was time for the adoption
ceremonies to begin.

With a promise to see him later and welcome him as
a brother, Chiksika left. Black Tooth, now brimming
with friendliness and laughing often, took Duke to the
riverbank where a large crowd had gathered. Once again
he told him to strip. This time Duke did not have as
much to remove; just a simple buckskin breechclout that
hung from his waist and a peculiarly comfortable pair of
slippers made of woven reeds.

When he was finished, Black Tooth grinned and
swatted him on the behind. "Wait here and just take
what comes," he said. He strode to a nearby *wegiwa,*
disappeared into it briefly, came out and walked toward
his own *wegiwa** not far from the *msi-kah-mi-qui.*

Duke's embarrassment over standing there naked became even worse when, a minute or two later, a trio of

* From *wegiwa* comes the familiar term, wigwam, which has
come to mean practically the same thing as teepee. They were
not the same. The Ohio Shawnees never lived in teepees. The
wegiwa was a square or rectangular structure of poles and treated
bark — nonportable, cool in summer, warm in winter, easily erected,
easily abandoned if the need came, yet stronger and roomier
than a teepee.

young squaws carrying paint pots left the first *wegiwa* and approached him. As he stood there stiffly, blushing deeply, they painted him all over with a variety of colors, giggling almost uncontrollably as they worked. As soon as they finished, however, they snatched up their paint pots and vanished in the crowd of amused onlookers.

Then Pucksinwah strode through the crowd to him. He was dressed in a simple but beautiful doeskin blouse and leggins. A cluster of five dark-brown, white-tipped eagle feathers were anchored to the back of his head and hung, tips down, over his right shoulder. The doeskin garments were so beautifully worked that they had become almost white, immaculately clean and so soft they were almost like velvet. A heavy necklace of hand-beaten silver encircled his neck and on his feet were buckskin moccasins sewn with designs of brightly colored beads and decorated with porcupine quills. And there was one other ornamentation he wore attached to his waist — a hoop to which were attached no less than a dozen scalps.

The chief's movements were graceful, almost catlike, giving the impression of great muscular strength and coordination always in reserve. He stopped several feet in front of Duke and raised both arms. The onlookers became silent and then Pucksinwah began the singsong chant of an ancient rite. The youth understood little of it, except for the last phrases, which were:

"... *Newecanetepa, weshemanitoo weshecatweloo, keweshelawaypa.*" — The Great Spirit is the friend of the Indians, let us always do good.

This ritual completed, Pucksinwah handed Duke into the care of three more squaws. These women were clad only in a type of pantaloon reaching from waist to knee. One was young and quite pretty, another middle-aged and with a stern expression. The third was a very old woman, entirely toothless and her face deeply wrinkled about the eyes and mouth with the lines of laughter.

The squaws led him into the water up to his waist, where they abruptly jumped upon him, pulling and tugging until he was knocked off balance and went under. The bottom here was more gravelly than muddy and, as he rose sputtering, they scooped up handfuls of fine pebbles and sand and scrubbed him with great energy. Not only was the paint rubbed away, but his skin became a bright pink from their scouring. Then he was permitted to return to shore.

During the early part of this washing many of the spectators had grunted and nodded approval, but soon they had begun drifting away and by the time the minor ordeal was over, most of the Indians had vanished. Black Tooth, however, had returned.

Still dripping and oddly refreshed, Duke was led by Black Tooth and followed by the squaws to the *msi-kah-mi-qui*. There they dressed him in a beautiful tasseled buckskin shirt, softer than any he had ever felt, and a pair of heavier buckskin leggins decorated with beads and ribbons, porcupine quills and hanks of red hair.

Once again his face was painted, but this time with care. On his cheeks and forehead, across nose and chin, were painted lines and spots of brilliant red, dull blue, deep yellow and pasty white. The thick black hair at the back of his head was woven through the perforations of a thin metal disc the diameter of a walnut. Into a small hole in its center they inserted an eagle feather so that it projected down at an angle, its tip resting across his right shoulder.

As this was being done the Indians — over six hundred men from Kispoko Town, Cornstalk's Town and Non-hel-e-ma's Town, entered the *msi-kah-mi-qui* clad in their finest and sat cross-legged on the floor of beaten earth. They whispered and smiled and now and then pointed toward him.

The voices stilled suddenly as Pucksinwah came in. Following him was his second-in-command, Chief She-me-ne-to — Black Snake — and behind him was Chiksika. As the three took their places in the center of the room close to where Duke was sitting beside Black Tooth, Chiksika flashed a quick bright smile and gave Duke a little nod. Duke returned the greeting.

At a wave of Pucksinwah's hand, the three squaws still hovering close to Duke scurried down the narrow aisle and out the door, dropping a thick buffalo hide into place behind them. There was now a heavy stillness in the dim room.

The chief of the Kispokotha Shawnees arose from where he had seated himself and walked over to Duke. He took the youth's hand and led him to the bearskin upon which he, Black Snake and Chiksika had been sitting. At a motion of the chief's head, Duke sat beside Chiksika and Pucksinwah himself sat in the center.

The war chief then handed Duke a pipe tomahawk decorated with blue-tinted feathers, a small bag containing punk, flint and steel for firemaking, and a pouch made of the entire pelt of a skunk which had been skinned pocket fashion. The tail hung down beneath it and the white stripes on the back rose and converged at the mouth of the pouch. This bag was filled with *kinni-kinnick*, the shredded and dried leaves of tobacco, sumac, willow and dogwood combined in an aromatic blend.

Pipes similar to the one the chief had given him were now being lighted all over the room. At a nod from Pucksinwah, Duke filled his with the *kinnikinnick*. Then he ignited his punk with the flint and steel and with this lighted his pipe and puffed shallowly. Until every pipe had been smoked out and placed on the floor beside its owner, not a word further was spoken by anyone. By that time the room had taken on a bluish haze from the smoke but, to Duke's surprise, it was not at all unpleasant.

At last Pucksinwah rose from his sitting position. He looked to right and left, and there was the feeling that he had managed to look directly and deeply into the eyes of everyone present. He spoke then in a strong measured tone, clearly audible to everyone assembled here.

"My son, you are now flesh of our flesh and bone of our bone. By the ceremony which was performed this day, every drop of white blood was washed out of your veins; you are taken into the Shawnee nation and initiated into a warrior sept; you are adopted into a great family and now received with great seriousness and solemnity in this room and presence and place of a great man."

Marmaduke felt overwhelmed and close to tears.

"After what has passed this day," Pucksinwah continued, "you are now one of us by an old strong law and custom. My son, you have now nothing to fear — we are now under the same obligations to love and defend one another; therefore you are to consider yourself as one of our people and forever more to be known and respected as Weh-yah-pih-ehr-sehn-wah."

Blue Jacket!

Saturday, June 5, 1773

His life among the Shawnees was everything Blue Jacket had hoped it would be and even more. He had adopted the Indian life every bit as completely as the Indians had adopted him. Rare were the times now when he thought of himself as ever having been a white boy named Marmaduke Van Swearingen. Nor had any of the Kispokotha Shawnees, since the day of his adoption ceremony nearly two years ago, ever again mentioned the fact that he was white.

In truth, their belief in the adoption rite was so strong that to each and every one of them, Blue Jacket was an Indian; just as much a Shawnee as Chiksika, Black Tooth, Black Snake or even Pucksinwah himself. To the tribe's way of thinking, Blue Jacket was born a

Shawnee on the day of his adoption and he had no life previous to that. And, though it was more difficult for him, even Blue Jacket himself was coming to feel this way.

In the two years since he had left his white background behind him, he had adapted himself unusually well to the social, moral, political and religious beliefs and customs of the Shawnees. In all cases he considered them far superior to those of the whites — simpler and more honest.

Within eight or nine months he had become so fluent in the Shawnee tongue that he had no difficulty understanding even the concepts of Indian mythology, or in making himself understood in any matter he wished to discuss. And now, after two years, without even realizing it, he was even thinking in Shawnee terms and in the Shawnee tongue.

Sharp of mind, quick of body, generous, even-tempered and considerate, Blue Jacket soon became extremely popular. He entered all the sports, habits, games and labors of his fellows with such enthusiasm and cheerfulness and with such respect for others that he began to have a considerable following. More and more frequently he was invited to take part in the sept and tribal councils.

Much of the credit for this had to go to Pucksinwah himself, who spent many hours and days instructing him in the history and culture of the Shawnees and in the religion which played such an important part in their lives. In his white life, the youth had hated school in general and history in particular, but this was something different and he virtually ate it up.

Pucksinwah taught him the history, traditions and codes of the tribe strictly by word of mouth, since nothing was written. Nor was it enough that he merely be told of these matters; he must, as was custom, commit them to memory so perfectly that he could repeat them exactly, with nothing added, changed or left out. Only in this way could the tribe's history be passed accurately from one generation to another.

"The Supreme Being of All Things," Pucksinwah told him, "is Moneto. It is Moneto himself who rules *ya-la-ku-qua-kumi-gigi* — the universe — and He dispenses His blessings and favors to those who earn His goodwill, just as He brings unspeakable sorrow to those whose conduct merits His displeasure.

"Moneto," the chief added, "is not to be mistaken for the Great Spirit, or ruler of destinies, who is subordinate to Him. The Great Spirit, whose name is Inu-msi-ila-fe-wanu, is a grandmother who is constantly weaving an immense net which is called a *skemotah*. When this net is finished it will be lowered to the earth and all who have proven themselves worthy will be gathered into its folds and taken to a world of great peace and happiness. At the same time, an unspeakably terrible fate will overtake the rest as the world comes to an end. Good conduct always brings reward, just as evil conduct must bring sorrow.

"No one," Pucksinwah continued, "is forced to believe in these matters, Blue Jacket. Force is not necessary. We know them to be truth. Morality is a fixed law, but each of us is his own judge. From earliest childhood this is instilled in our minds, just as we are taught that deceitfulness is a crime of itself. We live according to our standards and principles, not for what others might think of us. Absolute honesty toward others of our tribe is the basis of character. The standards of conduct are strictly followed."

Pucksinwah's voice was gentle and compelling and Blue Jacket found himself hanging on every word the chief uttered. Everything he said seemed to be so logical and clear.

"The foundation of our existence," Pucksinwah said slowly, "is this: *Do not kill or injure your neighbor, for it is not him that you injure, you injure yourself. But do good to him, therefore add to his days of happiness as you add to your own. Do not wrong or hate your neighbor, for it is not him that you wrong, you wrong yourself. But love him, for Moneto loves him also as He loves you.*"

There was no such thing as a jail among the Shawnees, Blue Jacket learned, but misdeeds did not go unpunished. The punishments were of many kinds and determined by the type of offense. The chief's word was absolute law and any persistent refusal to obey him or the unwritten code of honorable conduct was punishable by severe flogging, or even death. Anyone refusing voluntarily to take his punishment like a man was exiled from the tribe, and to a Shawnee this was a fate much worse than execution. Nor were the women of the tribe free from the law. The most dreadful crime of which any woman could be convicted was *pockvano-madee-way* — gossip about people.

Blue Jacket was very impressed at the many points of similarity between the Shawnee religion and Christian-

ity. The greatest single difference was that his people —
and he now firmly considered the Shawnees to be his
people — believed they were responsible only for their
conduct toward their own race. To other races they
owed nothing, except to return the same treatment they
received.

Pucksinwah was not the only instructor Blue Jacket
had. Almost everyone he encountered was more than
willing to help him learn the Shawnee ways. Men such
as Black Snake and Black Tooth and Muga — the Bear
— went out of their way to help him, and even from
Chiksika, two years younger than himself, he learned a
great deal.

What Chiksika had learned in the years with his
father, he made every effort to pass on to Blue Jacket. He
taught him keenness of observation and how to bear pain
without grimace. He taught him how to bear loss without depression, danger without fear and triumph without pride. Most of all, he taught him mastery of self; the
need to control and direct his passions and not let them
rule him.

Together they fished in the streams and roamed
through woods and fields. With other youngsters they
learned the methods of making war, of stealthy approach, of ambush and of fierce attack against forces
much larger in numbers. Chiksika taught him the art of
tracking, stalking and hunting game, building traps and
deadfalls and snares. And he taught him how to accurately foretell the weather, the names of plants and trees,
birds and four-legged animals. He showed him how to
find roots that were edible and what plants could cure

illnesses or blunt the knife of pain. He learned the names and meanings of the thirteen moons of the Shawnee year and that each year began in spring with the Green Moon.

From Pucksinwah's wife, Methotasa, and from their lovely daughter, Tecumapese, he learned the value of patience and the need to have pity for those unfortunate or in his power. They taught him the essentials of honesty — especially honesty to self — in all matters and the value of speaking truth at all times. Cruelty for the sake of cruelty, whether to animals or to man, degraded a person. The man who cheated or stole or lied could never secure the most priceless possession of a Shawnee — honor among his fellows and in his own soul.

The most important lesson of all, taught him by everyone, was that of respect for his elders; a trait which went hand in hand with respect for authority. This meant not only respect for one's parents and chief, but for any person of the tribe who began to show advanced years. Such people always assumed some degree of importance and authority. And when talking was engaged in, whether in councils or just around the campfires, it was always the older people who spoke first and they were listened to carefully and their wisdom and advice deeply respected. Having respect for the aged became second nature to Blue Jacket.

All of this was tremendously interesting to him, but what fascinated him most were the occasional tribal councils which were called and to which twice now he had accompanied Pucksinwah.

These councils were held in the principal village of

the Chalahgawtha sept — the village called Chillicothe
on the banks of the Little Miami River.* This was where
Black Fish was chief, and Black Fish was also second
principal chief of the whole Shawnee nation, under
Hokolesqua — Cornstalk.

To these grand councils came the chiefs, subchiefs
and braves of every sept. At each of the two such
meetings he had attended, Blue Jacket had estimated the
number gathered to be about five thousand.

These councils were deadly serious. Their business
affected the tribe as a whole and the problem confront-
ing them now was the gravest one they had ever encountered. For eighteen years now, tribal representatives had
been meeting here at intervals in an effort to decide what
the Shawnees, as a nation, must do about the white man.
Despite treaties forbidding it, the whites were crossing
the mountains to the east and spilling into the valleys of
the Monongahela and the Allegheny: a wave of white
settlers flooding the Shawnees' land, killing their game,
destroying their forests and fields.

No problem before had ever caused so wide a rift in
the tribe as this. In fact, it was such a serious problem
that it threatened to cause a permanent break in the
nation. Cornstalk, as principal chief, was backed up by
both the Chalahgawthas and Maykujays when he declared, "We had better make peace with the white
people, as they are outnumbering us and increasing fast.

---

* Site of present Old Town, Ohio, three miles north of present
Xenia, which is the seat of Greene County, Ohio. The Shawnee
village was near the junction of present Massie's Creek and the
Little Miami River.

It seems Moneto is with them. Let us make peace with them and be always in peace with them."

"No!" replied Pucksinwah for the Kispokotha sept, and he was echoed by the chiefs of the Peckuwe and Thawegila septs. "No! Let us *not* make peace with the white people. Let us defend our lands and fight them until one or the other of us is destroyed to the last man."

Pucksinwah shook his head sorrowfully and his gaze took in the whole assemblage. "To the very marrow of my bones I know there can never be a true peace between Indians and whites. As surely as summer follows spring, the whites will not stop at the river valleys of what they now call western Pennsylvania, but which was once *our* land and is no more. Inevitably they must spread down the Spay-lay-wi-theepi to settle in our great and sacred hunting grounds of Can-tuc-kee. Our tribe from the north and the Cherokees from the south might share the bounty of that land below our great river, but no tribe — or white man! — is permitted to take up residence there."

Pucksinwah now appealed to his thousands of listeners with all the directness and force that was in him. "My tribesmen, my brothers, have not over one hundred summers of friction between Indians and whites proved that nothing can be gained for us by talks of peace? The whites are always asking to talk peace and eager to make treaties, but whenever we have agreed and treaties have been signed and boundaries established in the past, have not these very whites treated us with loathing and humiliated us? And in every case, have they not broken the treaty boundaries almost immediately after they were established? Think, my brothers, and remember, and then talk not to me of peace with the white man!"

Blue Jacket was moved by the words of his chief, as were many others present. But although the last council had lasted for almost a month, no final decision had been made on the matter.

For his own part, Blue Jacket sided with Pucksin-wah. He realized, because of his white heritage, and because he knew what the whites were like, that his chief had spoken the truth. The white settlers *would* come, and nothing except a united Indian force facing them could possibly hold them back — perhaps not even that.

On the way back to Kispoko Town, Chiksika told Blue Jacket, "Father will never make peace with the whites, regardless of what the tribe does. He is my father and I will ride with him."

"And I, too," vowed Blue Jacket.

VI

Wednesday, March 16, 1774

Blue Jacket was deeply impressed by Tal-ga-yee-ta, the tall and angular Cayuga chief who was better known to both Indians and whites as Chief Logan. Logan was said to hold an incredible influence over the many tribes represented in this Northwest Territory, of which the Ohio country was part.

It had been no small honor that Pucksinwah had chosen Blue Jacket as one of the small number of Kispokothas to accompany him on this important mission to Logan. And also now they had arrived at Logan's little village on Yellow Creek in the far eastern portion of the Ohio country.* Here they had been warmly welcomed by Logan and a fine feast had been spread for them.

* The village was several miles upstream from where Yellow Creek empties into the Ohio River, which is two miles downstream from present Wellsville, Ohio.

As they went through these preliminaries before getting down to business, Blue Jacket reflected on the situation. Logan was extremely important to them, of this there was no doubt. Time and again his wisdom and persuasiveness had smoothed strained relationships between Indians and whites. He was well known and trusted by both races.

The stern-faced Shawnee delegation had not come because of Logan's peacemaking abilities, however. If they could convince him of the necessity of warding off the encroaching whites, he might be able to get the other tribes in the Ohio country to back up the Shawnees. One reason they felt Logan would be more than normally sympathetic to their views was because Logan's own wife was a Shawnee.

As Logan listened to them, his brow furrowed with concern. Pucksinwah was strong in his plea:

"Tal-ga-yee-ta, hear me; the white men over this year past have greatly increased their harassment of the Shawnees. At this time they are beginning to spread downriver toward the Can-tuc-kee hunting lands and from there they must soon cross north of the Spay-lay-wi-theepi to drive the Shawnees — as well as other tribes — from their villages.

"Some of the whites in the border areas," he continued, "have been disguising themselves as Indians in order to steal the horses or possessions of their fellow settlers, or even to kill them and take their scalps so that the blame will be fixed upon the Shawnees or other Indians.

"The Shawnees," he added proudly, "can fight their own battles with the whites, but the strong word of Tal-ga-yee-ta is needed to encourage the other tribes to stand fast and to stop, by battle if necessary, any whites crossing into the Ohio country. If they do so without opposition, we are lost, all of us. The Shawnees alone cannot — and should not! — be expected to guard the entire frontier for the benefit of all the Ohio tribes. Now there is word that the white fathers in the east are forming armies to come against the Shawnees and all tribes here must do their part to help stem this flood."

The reply of Logan was a bitter disappointment.

"Pucksinwah," said the Cayuga carefully, "you do me great honor coming here. The Shawnees are now and always have been my friends. Never, however, has Logan ever raised his hand against the whites; not even when some members of my own family have been slain in battle against them. There is no future in warring with a nation having unlimited resources and more men by far than all the tribes together."

A faint trace of a smile crossed his lips. "What's more, my friend," he added, "have not the Shawnees themselves been guilty of stealing horses and equipment from the whites on the borders? Have they not, when occasion prompted it, slain whites and taken scalps? Will defiance of the white men's armies make the threatened war wither and die, or will it instead cause violent and immediate retaliation against which there can be no standing?

"These, Pucksinwah, are the questions which touch me now," he said, and then continued in a more gentle tone, "The Shawnees are brave and their complaints are to large degree justified. But is it not better to attempt to reach an understanding? Is it not better to be guided by clear thought than by blind emotion? Surely there *must* be a way in which white men and Indians may live beside one another in peace and harmony, but this can never come to be without restraint on both sides. No, Logan will not raise a hand or voice against the whites, but this he *will* do: he will at once send emissaries to them and ask of them the same restraint that he is now asking of you."

His face expressionless, Pucksinwah argued no further. The council adjourned and, as Blue Jacket and the rest of the small party of Shawnees mounted their horses, the Kispokotha chief addressed the Cayuga chief one final time.

"Tal-ga-yee-ta is a wise man, but he must beware lest Matchemenetoo — the Bad Spirit — blind him to what is inevitable and one day he find himself and his people in grave danger from the white man. No, Tal-ga-yee-ta, there is not now, nor can there ever be, a true and equitable peace between Indian and white."

VII

Wednesday, April 27, 1774

The Kispokotha Shawnees had considered at length the words of Chief Logan and decided, for the time being at any rate, to use the restraint he had advised. Wherever possible, contact was avoided with the whites and the Shawnees kept strictly to their own side of the river they called Spay-lay-wi-theepi and the white men called the Ohio River. Pucksinwah continued to have grave doubts that following such a course would do the Shawnees much good. He was proved correct.

Blue Jacket was the first of the three-man Kispokotha hunting party to detect the camp of the whites as they followed a game trail along Pipe Creek.* He was startled at the surge of anger which filled him at witnessing the

* This camp was located near the mouth of Pipe Creek on the Ohio River, not far from the site of present Steubenville, Ohio.

invasion of these whites into the Ohio country. In a harsh whisper he now urged his companions that they circle the camp widely, unseen and unheard, and report the sighting to Pucksinwah.

The eldest of the trio was a thick-bodied Indian named Muga — the Bear. He carried a deep scar across his right temple where, as an infant, he had been clawed by the animal for which he was named. The other member of their party was a boy of seventeen named Aquewa Apetotha — Child-in-a-Blanket.

Muga brushed aside Blue Jacket's caution. "I think we should advance on the camp showing peaceable expressions," he said. "Perhaps we can thus encourage the same expressions among the whites. One cannot tell what great effect just such a simple meeting as this might have."

Against his better judgment, Blue Jacket let himself be convinced. They stepped out of cover into the clearing, their right hands raised in a sign of peace.

Almost instantly several shots rang out and both of Blue Jacket's companions fell without a sound. Blue Jacket himself ducked into a crouched run and plunged through the heavy cover of the forest. A delayed shot sent a lead ball buzzing angrily through the foliage over his head. He ran in a silent half-circle and within minutes was peering into the clearing from concealment on the opposite side to where he had first been seen.

A dozen men, dirty and rough-looking, were clustered around the two bodies. Aquewa Apetotha had already been scalped. Even as he watched, Blue Jacket saw Muga's scalp cut away by a grinning, bearded white man, who held it aloft in triumph and broke into what he must have thought was an Indian war dance but which looked more like an Irish jig.

Two other men ran up from the camp and a fierce argument arose and, though he could not clearly make out what they were saying, twice Blue Jacket heard one of the men addressed as Colonel Cresap. He shut his eyes and closed one ear with his hand so as to hear better. It had been so long since he had heard English spoken that it came to him as an ugly and alien sound.

The men began walking toward their camp, leaving the desecrated bodies sprawled behind. But before they got out of hearing, Blue Jacket caught the words "Logan" and "Yellow Creek" and ". . . kill them all."

He fled then, his passage more silent than the faint breeze. Within a quarter-hour he had returned to where the horses were hobbled and he caught all three. Then, riding his own mount and leading the other two, he struck out for the village of Chief Logan as rapidly as he could travel.

It was long after dark before he arrived there. He was thirsty and very weary, but this did not keep him from going at once to the dwelling of the chief. He was made welcome and Logan called for a pipe and food to be brought, but Blue Jacket shook his head impatiently.

"There is no time," he said. "White men, many of them, have just killed my companions, Muga and Aquewa Apetotha, on Pipe Creek. They scalped them. We had come in peace and they answered with murder. Before I left I heard them speak of coming here, to your village, to kill everyone!"

Logan looked concerned, but not as much as Blue

Jacket had expected. The chief shook his head. "I am sorry for you and for the death of your friends," he said sadly, "but you must have misunderstood what those men said. Perhaps your party gave them reason — without even realizing it," he added hastily, "— for what they did. It may be they thought you meant to attack."

Blue Jacket opened his mouth to deny this, but Logan appeared not to notice and went on. "The whites have been my friends, just as the Indian tribes have been. They have been welcomed into my village before this and they would have no reason now to attack me or my people. I am sure you must be mistaken, but I will prepare myself in any event. I am indebted to you for coming to tell me. My home is yours. Food and bed will be fixed for you."

Hardly able to contain his anger, Blue Jacket shook his head. "I cannot stay," he said tightly. "My chief must be told, as must the families of Muga and Aquewa Apetotha, so that they may begin to mourn their loss and prepare for vengeance. My own people," he added bitterly, "will believe what I have to say."

He left the chief then and outside encountered a squaw bringing food and drink to them. He took a gourd from her and drank deeply from it, then handed it back and walked quickly to his horses without a word. In a moment he cantered out of the village toward the far-distant Kispoko Town to the Southwest.

"Others may think him a wise man," he muttered in the darkness after a while, "but my own eyes have been opened. Tal-ga-yee-ta is a fool!"

VIII

There was no longer any doubt that war with the whites was very near. In the weeks and months following Blue Jacket's warning to Logan, matters had gone from bad to worse. It gave the young Shawnee no pleasure to know that Logan's blindness to the warning had resulted in a severe blow to him.

On April 30, three days after he had left Logan's Yellow Creek village, a party of white men had ambushed a large group of Logan's men, women and children. All but three of the Indians had been killed and among the dead were all the remaining relatives of the influential chief, including his brother, sister, father and brother-in-law. Even after they were dead or wounded, the most horrible atrocities had been committed upon their bodies. Logan's sister, for example, heavy with child, had tried to flee and was wounded with a bullet in her back. They had tied her by the wrists to a tree branch with her feet off the ground and then toma-hawked her.

When Logan himself, alerted by the three survivors, arrived on the scene the next morning, an overpowering rage struck him. He declared war against the whites, buried his dead and vowed he would not ground his tomahawk again until he personally had killed ten whites for every Indian who had fallen there. Then, to aid the Shawnees and also to have his remaining people protected by them, he moved to a place near Kispoko Town.

Killings became frequent in border skirmishes and an all-out war seemed inevitable. Then there was a sudden ray of hope. Cornstalk was invited to come to Fort Pitt, where the Monongahela and the Allegheny join to form the Ohio River, there to discuss a new treaty. But be-cause of high feelings running against the Indians, he was asked to come only with a small company instead of the usual large following for such affairs.

Cornstalk agreed and took with him only his younger brother, Silverheels, and his gigantic sister, Non-hel-e-ma, whom the whites knew as the Grenadier Squaw. But the three had no sooner arrived at Fort Pitt than a mob rushed them and Silverheels was stabbed deeply in the chest. Non-hel-e-ma and Cornstalk managed to escape, carrying their wounded brother, but from that instant on all hope of peace was shattered.

For his own part, Blue Jacket was eager for the war;

eager for a chance to retaliate for the murder of his two companions, and for an opportunity to drive the whites back across the Appalachians. Most of the younger braves, and many of the older ones, felt the same.

The first thrust of the army, however, came not at the Scioto River villages, but rather at the half-dozen villages collectively called Wapatomica. These were located far to the north and east of Kispoko Town, above the fork of the Muskingum River.

At the approach of General McDonald's army in midsummer, the entire population abandoned the towns and fled to the west. At the headwaters of the Mad River, close to the villages of the Maykujay Shawnees, they established a new Wapatomica. McDonald had had to content himself with merely destroying the deserted villages. Then he returned to Fort Pitt.

By the end of September the blood of many settlers and Indians had been spilled on the frontier and now an army of two divisions was advancing — this time against the Scioto River villages. One of the wings of the army was under Lord Dunmore, governor of the Colony of Virginia. It was presently floating down the Ohio, planning to join at Point Pleasant at the mouth of the Great Kanawha River with the southern wing of the army, led by Colonel Andrew Lewis. That was the situation when Chief Cornstalk called an early morning council of the Shawnees of the Scioto River villages.

It was a large council and an angry one. For the first time since he had become principal chief, Cornstalk's advice and counsel had been overruled. The stand he was taking was not a popular one — especially in view of what had happened at Fort Pitt.

Cornstalk had not become one of the great chiefs in Shawnee history by avoiding battle. He was, in fact, a daring and courageous leader who had often led his warriors on successful attacks against their enemies. But this time he urged his tribesmen to consider again what was in store and to make another effort to establish peace with the whites.

"We are eight hundred Shawnee warriors," he told them in this final council. "Even with the aid of our brothers, the Cayugas, Senecas, Delawares and Wyandots, we are only a thousand strong. The *Shemanese* — Long Knives — have three men or more to our one and their guns are newer and better. I ask you once again, think to the future of our race."

His plea made little impression. They had had enough of peacemaking. Now was a time of war and if Cornstalk would not lead them, then they would be led by Pucksinwah and Black Snake. There was no other way. Reluctantly Cornstalk agreed. For some hours after that they listened to reports of spies who had been watching both wings of the advancing army.

The white father, Dunmore, had the most men, but he was still far up the Spay-lay-wi-theepi at the white settlement that had first been called Zane's Station, but which had recently been renamed Wheeling. It would be many days before he could reach the Great Kanawha. On the other hand, the white warrior chief named Lewis was almost at that point already and his force was much smaller than Dunmore's; not much larger, in fact, than their own. In addition, a detachment of three hundred of Lewis's men was a full day behind the main thrust, bringing up the beef cattle and supplies. If the Indian force could strike while Lewis had only eight hundred men, it would have a distinct advantage, even though the army was far better armed.

Cornstalk listened carefully and then nodded and arose to speak a final time. "We will leave at once," he said, "to attack the *Shemanese* under Lewis, but remember this: now there will be no turning back; now the seed of war has been planted and watered and already it sprouts. Whether it thrives and grows or is cut down remains yet to be seen."

Within the hour they were riding southeastward through the hill country of Ohio along the trail which would take them directly to the mouth of the Great Kanawha. The large procession was led by three riders — Cornstalk in the middle, flanked on his left by the huge Non-hel-e-ma and on his right by Silverheels, who was still recovering from his wound but refused to be left behind.

A short distance behind these three rode Pucksinwah and his quiet but devoted lieutenant, Black Snake. Flanking this pair were two young men, their eyes alight with excitement and anticipation. It would be their first battle with the *Shemanese* and they were eager to prove themselves. To the left of the chief of the Kispokothas, tall and strong upon the back of a chestnut mare, rode his eighteen-year-old son, Chiksika.

And to the right of Black Snake, on a dappled gray, rode the remarkably well-muscled twenty-year-old called Blue Jacket.

IX

The crossing of the Spay-lay-wi-theepi had been done simply and silently, with no one in the enemy camp aware of what was happening. The Indian force had arrived just after dark last night at the river and a thousand pairs of eyes peered from cover at the crude fortification that had been thrown together by the weary army.

A whispered council was held and a plan agreed upon by the principal battle chiefs — Cornstalk, Pucksinwah, Logan, Black Snake, Red Hawk, Wolf and Elinipsico, the son of Cornstalk. They would move upriver a mile, and cross over silently in the light bark canoes that had been carried along strapped between horses, each craft capable of ferrying ten men at a time.

The position of the army on the triangular point of
land would make it difficult to attack. With the Kanawha
and Spay-lay-wi-theepi joining behind them, it would be
next to impossible to flank them, meaning a frontal attack would be necessary. The attack would begin at
dawn and with Moneto at their sides to protect and
guide them, the Indians were confident they would wipe
out the whole force.

As the first gray light of morning began outlining the
hills behind them, the line of a thousand painted warriors began creeping forward. Instants later a gunshot
sounded as a sentry fired at an Indian and missed, but
paid with his life for it as several balls struck him in
return.

There was frantic activity in the camp as Colonel
Andrew Lewis ordered a counterattack in three wings,
leading the center himself. The Kanawha side was led by
his brother Charles, and the Ohio side by James Fleming, both of whom were colonels, too. The lines were
hastily formed and moved out abreast to meet the
Indians.

The scattered firing suddenly turned into a wild barrage and in this first firing Colonel Charles Lewis was
killed as a ball tore through his skull. At almost the same
time, on the other end of the line, Colonel Fleming was
put out of action when a shot passed through his body
just beneath the ribs.

The first onslaught of the Indians was strong and
broke the line of the defenders, forcing them to give
ground for some minutes until they took cover behind

logs, trees, rocks or anything else that might provide protection from the withering fire.

Back and forth through the morning hours the battle
raged, first the whites giving ground, then the Indians.
Never before had Blue Jacket felt so alive, so powerful,
so filled with lust for blood. Before him and behind and all
around there was an incredible din — a rising and falling
chorus of screams and harsh cries, gunfire and grunts,
curses and moans. The acrid gunsmoke was thick
now and lay close to the ground, hiding both friends and
enemies in a blue-white screen. The eyes of everyone
streamed tears as they blinked against the burning it
caused. Bodies lay everywhere.

After firing his flintlock only twice, Blue Jacket threw
the clumsy weapon aside and relied on his bow until his
quiver was empty. Few of his arrows missed their mark.
When they were gone he discarded bow and quiver and
darted about, tomahawk in one hand and knife in the
other, engaging each white he encountered in mortal
combat.

Five, six, seven times he left behind him the bodies of
militiamen, pausing only an instant after each had fallen
to cut off the scalp and scream in triumph and defiance.
A bullet had grazed his neck, and the blood streaming
down his broad chest and back, mingling with the black
and white paints with which he had decorated himself,
gave him the appearance of some fantastic devil. More
than one white man dropped his weapon and fled in
panic when Blue Jacket loomed before him.

Pucksinwah and Chiksika fought side by side in the
first battle father and son had ever shared. But just be-

fore noon a bullet smashed into the war chief's breast
and felled him. Stunned, Chiksika cradled his father's
head and wept unashamedly. With his dying breaths,
Pucksinwah spoke faintly:

"Chiksika . . . your turn now . . . head of family.
Preserve its . . . its honor and dignity. . . . Never give
in to . . . whites. Teach Tecumseh . . . triplets . . .
ways of war . . . courage . . . stamina . . . ability in
. . . in battle. Prov— . . . provide for . . . mother
. . . and . . . sist—"

He wheezed faintly and relaxed in death.

All morning long up and down the line could be
heard the deep, powerful voice of Cornstalk, urging his
warriors on with praise where they were fighting well,
rallying them where they were weakening with cries of
"Oui-shi-cat-to-oui! Oui-shi-cat-to-oui!" — Be strong! Be
strong!

Still weak from the chest wound suffered at Fort Pitt,
Silverheels fought doggedly near his brother until he collapsed with exhaustion and was picked up and carried
out of the battle area by the only woman who fought
there, six-and-a-half-foot Non-hel-e-ma.

For five hours they fought at a feverish pitch, within
a line less than two hundred yards deep and along a
front of a mile and a quarter. Occasional firing came
after that, but not a great deal. Still the smoke hung
heavily and the crouching soldiers prayed for a breeze to
sweep it away so that they might be able to see their
foe.

But word had come to Cornstalk now that the three-
hundred-man rear guard was coming up rapidly and he

sent runners to pass the word to withdraw. So they did, under cover of the smoke screen, taking along with them all of their dead and wounded.

It was early evening when the rear guard arrived and Colonel Andrew Lewis mounted an attack. By then, however, not an Indian remained on his side of the river. The soldiers were jubilant at what they quickly began calling their "victory."

But this so-called victory was a hollow one indeed. They had lost more than half of their officers and fifty-two militiamen, for a total of seventy-five men dead. There were also a hundred and forty men injured, of whom eighty-eight would do no more fighting.

The Indians, on the other hand, had a total of twenty-two killed and only eighteen wounded, of whom only five were so badly wounded they would not fight again.

All the way back to Kispoko Town, Chiksika rode with his dead father cradled in his arms. Though the tears were gone now, his face was frozen in an expression of deep inner pain. Close beside him, ready to help should the arms of his young companion begin to fail, rode Blue Jacket.

And his cheeks were still wet.

Thursday, November 10, 1774

A month had passed since that single battle in what was now being called Lord Dunmore's War. There might well have been more, but the war fever that had filled many of the Indians before that fight at Point Pleasant cooled off quickly during the ride back to the Scioto villages.

Hardly had they returned across the Spay-lay-wi-theepi and begun the return, in fact, than the allies of the Shawnees deserted them. Without council with Cornstalk, without even a word of explanation, the Mingoes, Delawares and Wyandots abruptly broke away from the procession and struck out for their own home areas by different routes, looking fearfully over their shoulders for pursuers.

This was an act of thorough cowardice and desertion. They were, in a manner of speaking, throwing the Shawnees to the wolves. Dunmore's army, nearly three times as large as that of Lewis, was camped at the mouth of the Hockhocking River* and prepared to thrust directly westward to the Scioto villages. Lewis's army would sweep up from the south to meet Dunmore there. The villages of the Wyandots, Mingoes and Delawares were more distant and out of the path of the army. It was the Shawnees, therefore, who would now have to bear the brunt of the retaliation.

A great contempt filled Cornstalk. He did not bid them stay, nor did he call them cowards, but their eyes dropped before his cold gaze. They rode away with a permanent cloak of shame over their shoulders. Only Logan, of them all, remained to stand by the Shawnees in whatever should come now.

Cornstalk permitted no stopping until the Scioto villages were reached, but his disgust and contempt turned to anger as he heard his own warriors behind him speaking not of further battle, but of suing for peace before the army should close upon them and crush them.

Black Snake, riding close to Chiksika and Blue Jacket, had been openly scornful of the "frightened quail" riding behind them and as angry with them as was Cornstalk. He shot a glance at Blue Jacket and his voice was bitter. "And are you, like these others, trembling with fear at what might come now?"

Blue Jacket's gaze locked on that of the new chief of

---

* Now known as the Hocking River.

the Kispokotha Shawnees, which was what Black Snake had become with the death of Pucksinwah. The young man was desperately weary but his own voice was firm and full of conviction.

"I do not dream of peace," he said quietly. "Pucksinwah said many times there could never be peace between Indians and whites. He was right. I will fight beside you, Black Snake, as long as there is breath in me to fight. And should you be killed before me, I will still continue to fight to the end."

Chief Black Snake merely grunted, but in his eyes was reflected a deep respect for Blue Jacket. In the battle he had seen him rush ahead where other Kispokothas had fallen back. He had seen him strike one enemy after another, exulting in the battle and exhibiting a fierceness he had rarely witnessed in another. Blue Jacket was an outstanding warrior.

But the personal desire to fight on was taken out of their hands. Cornstalk had called for a general council meeting immediately upon their return to the villages. The gathering was strangely subdued.

"You have fought well, my children," the principal chief told them, "and the heart of Hokolesqua sings the song of praise for your strength in battle, just as it sings the song of mourning for our brave warriors and chiefs who fell. Now I must ask you, was this all in vain? A few of you have said you will fight on, but only a few. Many, many more have said 'Let us now seek peace with the *Shemanese* lest they come against us even more strongly.' My heart is filled with shame that my ears have heard these words. If it was peace you wanted, why did you not say so when I begged you to do so five days ago?"

He then asked loudly, angrily, "What do we do now? The *Shemanese* are coming upon us by two routes, far stronger than those we met alone, while we are weakened by the return of our brothers to their distant homes where they will be safe." The contempt was heavy in his voice and he went on after a brief pause: "So what do we do now? Shall we turn out and fight them? Shall we be men?"

In reply there was only an embarrassed shuffling and eyes which fell away from his stern gaze. At that, some vital spark seemed to go out of the chief. He drew out his bloodstained tomahawk and held it high for all to see, then hurled it savagely to the ground so that nearly the entire head was buried when it hit. In a voice thick with anger, frustration and shame he shouted, "Since you are not inclined to fight, we will go and make peace!"

At those words there had been a roar of approval and runners were dispatched at once to Dunmore with treaty proposals. Five days ago Cornstalk would have welcomed this, but now it was the saddest day of his life.

And so a new treaty had been drawn up and the army pulled back. It was a treaty, Black Snake warned darkly, which would cause the Shawnees great trouble. Although the whites agreed to stay out of the Ohio country, making the Spay-lay-wi-theepi the permanent boundary between Indians and whites, they demanded the right to come down the river to settle in the wild lands of western Virginia — the Can-tuc-kee lands, which were the sacred hunting grounds of the Shawnees. The Indians had had no choice but to agree and to further pledge that they would molest no whites traveling on the river. In return, the Indians were still to retain the right to cross the river and hunt in their traditional hunting grounds.

Blue Jacket had accompanied Cornstalk and Black Snake and the other chiefs and warriors who made up the delegation to seal the peace. Only Logan refused to attend, though he did dictate a speech to be read at the negotiations. It was a speech which had a great impact on both the Indians and whites attending the meeting. It was:

"I appeal to any white man to say if ever he entered Logan's cabin hungry and I gave him not meat; if ever he came cold or naked and I gave him not clothing. During the course of the last long and bloody war,* Logan remained idle in his lodge, an advocate for peace. Nay, such was my love for the whites that those of my own country pointed at me as I passed and said, 'Logan is a friend of the white man.' I had even thought to have lived with you, but for the injuries of one man. Colonel Cresap, the last spring, in cold blood and unprovoked, murdered all the relatives of Logan, not sparing even my women and children.† There runs not a drop of my

* Logan refers here to the French and Indian War, in which he refused to take part and acted as a peacemaker between Indians and whites.

† In this, Logan was mistaken. Colonel Michael Cresap and his men were not the whites who murdered Logan's family. The deed was done by a party of nearly thirty men led by two white men named Greathouse and Tomlinson.

blood in the veins of any living creature. This called on
me for revenge. I have sought it. I have killed many. I
have fully glutted my vengeance. For my country, I re-
joice at the beams of peace; but do not harbor the
thought that mine is the joy of fear. Logan never felt
fear. He will not turn on his heel to save his life. Who is
there to mourn for Logan? Not one!"

But sadness was not limited to Logan alone. All of
the Kispokothas mourned the loss of their great chief,
but the greatest grief filled the family of Pucksinwah —
and this included Blue Jacket. The grief was intensified
by the fact that now Pucksinwah's family would move
away to take up residence in Chillicothe among the
Chalahgawtha Shawnees, and become a part of the family of Chief Black Fish.

The oversight and care of a fallen war chief's family,
because of his rank and service, always became the
peace chief's duty until time and circumstance eased
their necessities. In effect, even though Methotasa would
still have no husband, her daughter and five sons would
have, in Black Fish, a father.

It was a sensible arrangement, but Methotasa with-
drew in her shroud of grief. Her life had been so much a
part of Pucksinwah's that when he died, something in
her died, too. She had never loved another man and she
never would. The flame that had lighted her life had
gone out.

The parting was a sad one, especially since Blue
Jacket was not going along with them. One by one he
embraced Methotasa, Chiksika, Tecumapese, Tecumseh
and the triplets — Kumskaka, Sauwaseekau and Lowaw-

luwaysica. He returned then to Chiksika and placed his hands on the younger man's shoulders. He said nothing, nor did Chiksika, but the bond of affection which flowed between them spoke louder than words. They were brothers and, though now distance would separate them, they would be bound to one another for the rest of their lives.

The family was leaving Pucksinwah's Town forever, taking with them even the name of the village. Hereafter, even though it might still be called Kispoko Town, because it was the seat of the sept, it would no longer be known as Pucksinwah's Town. Now it would be known by the name of She-me-ne-to, the new chief of the Kispokotha sept; hereafter it would be called Black Snake's Town.

There was a good reason for Blue Jacket's staying behind, even though he had every right to go with the family of Pucksinwah. The Kispokotha sept not only had a new chief, it also had a new second-in-command — a strong, fierce, courageous warrior who had fought more vigorously than anyone else in the battle of Point Pleasant; a man who had won the respect and admiration of Chief Black Snake himself; a twenty-year-old warrior whose name was becoming widely known — Weh-yah-pih-ehr-sehn-wah.

XI

Saturday, July 2, 1775

A feeling of strong resentment and anger filled the gloomy silence of the huge *msi-kah-mi-qui* at the Little Miami River village of the Chalahgawtha Shawnees called Chillicothe. Blue Jacket was one of three hundred and fifty chiefs, subchiefs and delegates of the five Shawnee septs who waited quietly for Cornstalk to speak. As principal chief of the nation, Cornstalk would be next to last speaker. The honor of speaking last, however, would go to Black Fish of the Chalahgawthas, in whose council house this meeting was being held.

This *msi-kah-mi-qui* was one of the largest in the Shawnee nation, measuring fully a hundred and twenty feet in length by forty feet in width. Because of its spaciousness, the large number of people inside now seemed not quite as big a crowd as they actually were. More than once on other occasions councils here had included upwards of nine hundred people.

For many hours the chiefs assembled here had risen one by one to air their grievances and demand greater freedom to retaliate against the whites for the treatment they had been receiving from them. The trouble all seemed to stem from the peace treaty concluded with Lord Dunmore.

While this treaty supposedly still permitted no whites to cross the Spay-lay-wi-theepi into the Ohio country, it definitely opened wide the Can-tuc-kee lands to them. It had been the crumbling of a great dam which now permitted a flood of whites to swarm down the great river in every manner of floatable craft, from well-built boats to crude rafts.

The whites had come like a plague of locusts and wherever they stopped they cut down the trees and burned the prairies. Worse yet, in the sacred hunting ground of the Can-tuc-kee lands, the whites were slaughtering the elk and buffalo by the hundreds, often taking only the tongue or liver and leaving the rest of the carcass to rot. And they brought with them large herds of cattle and hundreds of horses which competed with the game for the food which grew there.

There were a great many noddings and grunts of approval when the war chief of the Shawnees finished his speech. Black Snake, who had been sitting on a buffalo rug beside Blue Jacket, had risen and spoke to the crowd not as the chief of the Kispokothas, but rather as the war chief of the entire tribe. His words had been angry and bitter.

"Only two full seasons have passed," he told them, "since the *Shemanese* came, but already the buffalo seem fewer and the elk have become solitary and always on the alert and difficult to down. But that is not the worst. The worst is the men themselves who float down the Spay-lay-wi-theepi and shoot to kill whenever one of us shows himself on our own shore."

Black Snake held up both his hands with the fingers spread and the thumb of one hand folded under. "Nine!" he said angrily. "Nine of our young warriors have been found dead on our shores since the Hunger Moon. Four of our men have crossed to the Can-tuc-kee lands to hunt meat and have never returned. White men have landed on our own shores and have tried to build cabins and have been angry with us when we tell them that they may not. They insult us and our wives and our children and our way of life. We are losing our dignity and our self-respect.

"Why," Black Snake demanded, "must it be *we* who turn our backs and walk away when it is *we* who are the injured? Why may we not, as we always have, repay in kind for what we receive at the hands of our enemies?"

There was mumbled conversation after he sat down again and even when Cornstalk stood it continued for a while as a gradually dying buzz. For long minutes the principal chief stood there without speaking, even after the chamber had become silent. At last his voice flowed out sad and soft, yet distinct to all who sat here.

"It is a bad time for us, yes. As with your war chief, She-me-ne-to, the fire in my breast also wishes to burst forth in vengeance for those crimes which have been committed against us. I hold back in this desire, for I have given my word, as have many of you here, that we will remain at peace."

His voice rose a little now. "Do not think now or ever that Hokolesqua so advises through fear, except that it is fear our nation will perish. If once again we begin war with the *Shemanese*, it will be the beginning of our end. The white man is like the worm who, when cut in half, does not die but merely becomes two. For each one of them that is killed, two or three or even four others rise to take his place."

Now he was appealing to their reason and trying to cool the hot emotions which filled them. "As the treaty last autumn opened the dam to let the whites down the river in a flood, so now will warfare against them be opening a dam to permit them to flood into our country here and take it from us. It is no easy matter to tell you that we must not fight, just as it is no easy matter to bear the injuries being turned upon us. Yet it may be that if these injuries can be borne for a while, better relationships will come and we will be able to live with the whites as neighbors."

Many of the older members of the tribe nodded and murmured in approval at these words, but the undertone of exasperation, disgust and anger became even greater from the younger men, especially those of the Chalahgawtha and Kispokotha septs. Blue Jacket himself felt revolted at the thought of any longer bearing the scorn and indignity, the injury and humiliation being heaped upon them by the whites. His voice was strong among those who growled with disfavor.

Cornstalk waited until the interior of the *msi-kah-mi-qui* quieted again and went on:

"Yes! The young men are hard to hold. They want to strike back when struck, and it is not in my heart to tell them they are wrong. They are *not* wrong! But look deep into your hearts, each of you, old men and young, and ask yourselves if any personal insult or injury is worth the destruction of our nation, which any retaliation now must surely bring."

With that, Cornstalk returned to his place beside Black Fish. As he sat down, the chief of the Chalahgawthas and of this village of Chillicothe arose. Black Fish was not a big man, even though well built. He was no more than five and a half feet tall. A queue of long, braided black hair hung from his head over his shoulder and down his chest, and a wide band of beaten silver encircled his left upper arm.

Black Fish was second in command to Cornstalk as principal chief of the Shawnee tribe and, as peace chief of the nation, it was expected that he would agree with the words of Hokolesqua. But now he surprised them. Tossing behind him the queue of hair hanging over his right chest, he tapped a finger to a large round scar that had been hidden by the braid. It was still an angry pink and not entirely healed and it looked like a medal on his chest.

"This is my memory," he said slowly. "It tells me that no white man can be trusted at any time, any place. It tells me that when I accepted injury and insult from the white man, believing it would not happen again, it became worse than before.

"The Shawnee," he cried, "must be able to live in dignity! He must not only demand respect of others, white or Indian, but, even more importantly, he must be able to retain his own self-respect. He can never do this by turning his back on injury and insult. My memory," he tapped the scar again, "tells me this."

He shook his head. "Hear me now! I do not say we should make war unless war is visited upon us, but I say we must protect ourselves. If our men are killed, we must kill. If our buffalo and elk and deer are destroyed, then so must the cows of the whites be destroyed and their horses taken from them. If our woods are cut down and our fields burned, then so must the cabins of the whites be burned. Only in this way will the *Shemanese* come to know that we will not allow our country to be ravished, our game to be slaughtered, our men to be killed, and they will think well on it before giving us further injury."

With that rousing declaration, Black Fish sat down and the large room virtually rocked with the whoops and howls of a large portion of the assemblage. Clearly the trend was toward instant retaliation. But even those who whooped now were sobered somewhat by the memory of what had been said earlier in the council by the oldest leader present. The chief of the Thawegila Shawnees, Ki-kusgow-lowa, had told them:

"The septs have always been joined closely together in all important phases of Shawnee life. Yet I tell you now that the Thawegilas have seen their last war with the *Shemanese*. If just once more the tomahawk is struck into the war post, the Thawegilas will leave the Shawnee nation and cross the great-grandmother of rivers to the west, never to return."

XII

Blue Jacket, visiting Chiksika in Chillicothe, was impressed with Tecumseh. For an eight-year-old, the boy was unusually tall, very erect, quite good-looking and remarkably intelligent. His abilities were apparent in whatever he engaged in and he considered it important to excel.

Tecumseh loved the games and sports in which he participated with his companions at Chillicothe and listened carefully to the lessons received from Chiksika and others who taught him. More than a few times Chief Black Fish had eyed the boy with pride and approval.

None of the other youngsters Tecumseh's age were any match for him and even those in early adolescence were hard put to keep up. His body was slim and solid and his impressive young muscles rippled beneath his skin as he ran or swam, jumped or wrestled with the others. The boy could ride a horse expertly and could shoot his little bow with the greatest of accuracy, even from astride his galloping mount.

"You have taught him well, Chiksika," Blue Jacket said. "Pucksinwah would have been proud of you both."

Chiksika smiled and was pleased, but argued that his part in Tecumseh's development was small. "One cannot teach a stone," he said. "It is Tecumseh who must have the credit. He is the leader in all he does and among all the boys. When sides are chosen in the games, it is he who is selected as leader and he always has a great company of companions about him, eager to follow him and do anything he suggests. And since you were last here, Blue Jacket, he has received his *Pa-waw-ka*."

Blue Jacket was glad to hear this and pressed Chiksika for the details. Chiksika obliged him. It had been a clear, crisp morning last October when, as foster-father, Black Fish had summoned Tecumseh. With solemn instructions the chief had informed him that it was now time for him to acquire his *Pa-waw-ka* — that is, to become owner of some material object through which he could approach and receive power from both Moneto and the Great Spirit in times of need. He was sent to Chiksika's *wegiwa* to strip himself, run naked from there to a deep hole in the nearby Little Miami River and plunge into it, then return and dress.

Each morning thereafter he was required to do this, right into the bitterest weather of the winter. As tem-

peratures fell and snow covered the fields, the task
became harder and harder to bear. Often he was forced
to break a skim of ice in the stream before he could take
his plunge. The frigid water and freezing air were a
severe test of willpower and endurance, but his obedience had remained unshaken. He was being disciplined
in obedience and reverence for the command of his
earthly father, to make him worthy of receiving the protection and loving care of Moneto and the Great Spirit.

In mid-January, on the morning of his final plunge,
Tecumseh was informed by Black Fish that the time of
preparation was at an end. He must now seek his *Pa-
waw-ka* symbol. He told the boy that this time he must
dive deeply to the very bed of the river, and there to
close his outstretched hands over whatever they
touched. Without looking at what he grasped in his
hands, he was to return to Black Fish.

This he did and, as he stood shivering with cold and
anticipation, the chief pried open one hand and found
some gravel and a piece of waterlogged twig. In the
other there was a soggy leaf and some sand and a piece
of white quartzite rock.

Black Fish took the rock between his fingers and held
it up. It was about the size of a pigeon's egg. He in-
spected it closely, turning it over several times and then
he grunted approvingly.

"This," he had told the boy, "is forever your *Pa-waw-
ka*, to be carried by you and used as an intermediary
between yourself and Moneto and the Great Spirit when
you are in need of help and direction. It will help pro-

vide you with courage and stamina and, most of all, with wisdom."

It had taken Tecumseh weeks to chip a groove all the way around the stone so that he might tie it securely and wear it around his neck. He was sure that wherever it touched his skin it gave off an inner warmth.

"It is well," Blue Jacket said, nodding. He congratulated Tecumseh, who smiled shyly and then ran outside. "And now," said Blue Jacket, turning back to Chiksika, "what is next for him?"

Chiksika's own smile faded. "What is next has already begun. I have started to train him in the matters of warfare."

Blue Jacket grunted. That was good. Relationships with the whites had gone from bad to worse. With the outbreak of warfare among the whites themselves, no longer were the Shawnees able to cross the river openly to hunt. Those who did so were shot from ambush. But for such acts the whites had recently been paying a heavy price. Though still advised not to do so by their older and more conservative chiefs, the young warriors had begun taking life for life, and in this they were being encouraged by British traders and Indian agents, who supplied them with guns and ammunition for this purpose. Thus, when Shawnees were killed, so were white men. When elk and buffalo were butchered, so were cattle. When forests were felled and fields burned, cabins became ashes.

Time after time Blue Jacket had crossed the river and time after time he had come close to losing his life. Already no less than a dozen settlers and border-roaming frontiersmen had fallen beneath his knife or tomahawk or gun. He was becoming known and deeply feared by the whites in the land which they were now calling Kentucky.

Attacks against the settlements were becoming more organized and in the past three or four months Blue Jacket had led several of them. And the whites themselves were forming armed groups which could rise at a moment's notice to give pursuit under such leaders as Daniel Boone, Simon Kenton, John Todd and James Harrod.

"It is well," Blue Jacket told Chiksika for the second time. "There is not real war yet, but as surely as winter follows summer, it must come before long."

XIII

Friday, October 10, 1777

The outbreak of full-scale hostilities began with the death of one man, Chief Pluk-kemeh-notee. The whites called him Pluggy and he was well known and greatly hated south of the Spay-lay-wi-theepi. He had an uncanny knack for moving about unseen among the white settlements and picking off stray settlers here and there, but more often merely taking horses and bringing them back to Chillicothe. He was a dour old man, short-tempered and fierce, and he hated all whites passionately. He had good reason; his wife and twelve-year-old son had been shot to death by a boatload of passing whites.

Third chief of Chillicothe, he had taken a retaliatory party across the river and attacked the little settlement of McClelland's Station.* In the brief skirmish, John McClelland had been killed, but Pluk-kemeh-notee had also taken two bullets in his chest and died.

As soon as news reached him of this, Black Fish called a council of the warriors of Chillicothe. He told them that Cornstalk had said they must not provoke war and that they must continue to honor the treaty with Dunmore. But now, with the death of one of their own chiefs, it had become a personal affront to the warriors of the village of Chillicothe, a matter which must be settled by them without delay. It was a sept matter, not a tribal one, so only Chalahgawtha warriors would participate. There was but one exception: Blue Jacket, second chief of the Kispokothas, who was visiting here in Chillicothe, would go along at his own request.

Black Fish told the council that they would leave with a force of two hundred warriors and would try to destroy every settlement in the Can-tuc-kee lands, of which there were now more than a dozen.

The attack began on March 6. Already many of the smaller stations in Kentucky had been abandoned and their residents had congregated at the three strongest forts — Boonesboro, Harrodsburg and Logan's Station, which was also called St. Asaph.† Small parties of Indians went from station to station, burning the deserted

* The site of present Georgetown, Kentucky.

† St. Asaph was founded and named by Benjamin Logan, but many people called it Logan's Fort after him. When it failed to fall to the Indians under their concerted attack, both Indians and whites began calling it Standing Fort. This name stuck, but has since been shortened to the present name of the city, Stanford, Kentucky.

buildings and destroying what cattle had not been taken along by the fleeing settlers. But it was against the three principal strongholds that their greatest fury was unleashed.

These forts were all kept under siege, and any person who ventured forth took his life in his hands. Days turned into weeks and weeks into months. Dozens of white men were injured, including Daniel Boone whose leg was broken by a bullet. At least twelve of the defenders were killed. So far as was known, no more than three or four Indians had been killed.

The most successful single attack came at St. Asaph on the next to the last day of the siege. Blue Jacket led the attack, catching by surprise seven people in the cattle compound outside the fort. All seven were killed and, after darkness had fallen, they were scalped.

There was a good chance that he could take the fort now, for only a handful of defenders remained inside to fight them off. But then runners came from Black Fish instructing Blue Jacket to withdraw and join with his party, and the Kispokotha did so.

So it was that on June 1, Black Fish assembled all his men and headed north to cross the Spay-lay-wi-theepi and go home to Chillicothe. The chief was not fully satisfied with the results of his expedition, but he was not especially disappointed either.

All but those three white settlements in the Can-tuc-kee land had been destroyed. Chief Pluk-kemeh-notee's death had been avenged many times over and perhaps the three months of continuous siege and harassment would show the settlers that no longer would the Shawnees step back and allow themselves to be injured in any way.

But the whole affair had an unexpected and tragic result. Returning to Black Snake's Town on the Scioto in late June, Blue Jacket at once crossed the river and told Cornstalk what had occurred. Cornstalk was deeply concerned and, with Blue Jacket at his side, immediately set out for the chief villages of all the septs, telling them that they must now prepare for drastic retaliation from the whites. He saw no way now that war could be avoided. He did not condemn Black Fish for his independent action but, in fact, commended him, saying he would have done the same.

More than anything else, however, Cornstalk was an honorable man and when the pair returned to the Scioto River villages, he announced his intention of visiting Fort Randolph, built on the site where they had fought the battle of Point Pleasant. There he would tell its commander that the peace treaty could no longer be honored. Did Blue Jacket wish to come along?

Blue Jacket declined the invitation. He wanted no contact with the race he had come to despise. Thus Cornstalk set off only with his son, Elinipsico, and his village subchief, Red Hawk. They arrived at Fort Randolph under a flag of truce on the third anniversary of the battle that had occurred here. They were shown to the quarters of the commander, Captain Arbuckle.

"I come with grave news," Cornstalk said slowly. "Three years ago I gave my word as principal chief of the Shawnees that our tribe would keep the peace, would remain on its own side of the river except to hunt, and would refrain from retaliation if grievances arose between my people and yours. This was a talk-treaty and the papers were to be marked later at the fort of Pitt. But that meeting never came about because of the war of revolution your own people are now fighting.

"I have come here to say to you that the grievances have become too great to be borne. I can no longer restrain my young men from joining the raiding parties encouraged by our friends, the British. I no longer *wish* to restrain them. We have suffered much at the hands of intruding whites, who have repeatedly broken the treaty. Now we have attacked the Can-tuc-kee settlements and there is a treaty no longer. It is a matter of honor that we have come here to tell you this."

Captain Arbuckle arose from behind his desk and, without a word to the chief, motioned to the small squad of soldiers standing along the wall. "Take them," he said. "Apparently we're at war with the Shawnees again. We'll hold these three as hostages."

Perplexed at the ways of white men, Cornstalk and his two companions allowed themselves to be flanked and then led to a small room in which there were only three narrow slits for windows.

The news of the imprisonment of this great chief who had led the Indians in the battle of Point Pleasant spread rapidly through the garrison. In a short time angry voices were calling back and forth. Suddenly the three captive Indians heard a door roughly pushed open and numerous heavy footfalls approaching. Cornstalk placed his hand on Elinipsico's shoulder.

"My son," he said gently, "the Great Spirit has seen

fit that we should die together and has sent you to that end. It is His will, and so let us submit."

The three of them stood erect and calmly faced the door. In a moment it was swung open fiercely and a mixed group of soldiers and frontiersmen armed with rifles crowded the entrance.

"By God," said Captain John Hall, "it *is* Cornstalk!"

He flung his weapon to his shoulder and fired. Instantly the other guns belched flame and smoke and even when the three Shawnees had crumpled to the floor in death, more shots came as men eager to do their bit in "fighting the enemy" shot at the corpses.

So fell Cornstalk, principal chief of the Shawnee nation, with no less than nine bullets in his body.

And so ended any pretense of peace between the races.

XIV

Sunday, February 8, 1778

Blue Jacket's current expedition south of the Spay-lay-wi-theepi with a hundred Chalahgawthas under his command was designed primarily to take as many horses as possible from the whites. He also wanted to gain information on the government forces which had arrived in the Can-tuc-kee lands since the siege last year.

They had followed the Licking River upstream from where it emptied into the Spay-lay-wi-theepi.* They were just reaching the Blue Licks, a well-known salt-lick area where once game had congregated in abundance, when Blue Jacket caught a glimpse of a white man heading their way, dressed in buckskin and carrying a rifle.

The party melted into the underbrush at a signal

---

* Site of present Covington, Kentucky, directly across the Ohio River from present Cincinnati, Ohio.

from Blue Jacket. Almost as if it had been planned, the man walked right up to them and then abruptly found himself surrounded. Realizing that he had no chance whatever for escape or defense, the frontiersman dropped his rifle and surrendered.

Blue Jacket sent out some scouts to backtrail the white man; then he led him to a tree and motioned for him to sit down. For a long while then, Blue Jacket merely stared down at him and the frontiersman, with no sign of fear, calmly stared back.

It had been a long time since Blue Jacket had spoken or even thought in English and now, as he spoke it for the first time in well over six years, it was strange on his tongue and his sentences were poorly formed and halting. The frontiersman assumed he was an Indian who had learned English rather than a white man who was out of practice.

"Who are you?" the chief asked, breaking his silence.

Surprised, the white man grinned faintly and said, "They call me Boone. Dan'l Boone."

Boone! The incredible frontiersman who had been such a thorn in their sides and who had eluded them for so long. Blue Jacket could not have been more pleased with the capture of George Washington. He questioned the frontiersman at length and Boone answered casually.

"What are you doing here?" Blue Jacket asked.

"Hunting," Boone said, nodding his head toward his rifle, now being held by a young warrior. "Meat hunting, for all the new soldiers that are at St. Asaph and Harrodsburg and Boonesboro. Takes ten-fifteen hunters like me jest to keep 'em in meat."

Blue Jacket frowned. "Soldiers? How many?"

"Don't rightly know fer sure," Boone replied carelessly. "Ain't never counted 'em. 'Spect there must be four-five thousand of 'em now, though."

Realizing Boone was lying, Blue Jacket cuffed him smartly across the face and repeated the question. Boone's lip was cracked and he spat some blood out. "They's enough to kill ever' Injen 'twixt here an' Deetroit," he said.

Blue Jacket chuckled. This man didn't scare easily. But he didn't lie well, either. He continued to fire questions at him, but the answers weren't very satisfactory. Then one of his scouts raced up and spoke rapidly in Shawnee.

"White men," he said. "Twenty-seven of them. They are making salt at the licks. I followed this one's tracks to them."

"Guns?" Blue Jacket asked quickly.

The warrior shrugged. "A few. Maybe eight or nine. Two or three guards out. That's all."

Blue Jacket squeezed his shoulder and nodded. "Good." He turned back to Boone. "All you have said has been lies, Boone. You are from the salt makers. It is for them you are hunting meat."

Boone merely looked at him and Blue Jacket was tempted to hit him again, but restrained himself. "We are going to take them," he told the frontiersman. "Whether alive or dead is up to you. You will go in and tell them to lay down their arms and surrender to us."

"Don't figger too much on me doin' that," Boone said. "It ain't likely."

"More likely than you think. We will surround the

salt camp unseen, our guns at ready. At least two rifles will be aimed at every man there. Then we will send you in. You have a choice of telling them to surrender or all will be killed instantly. My own gun and several others will be aimed at you."

Boone knew now that he had no choice but to do as Blue Jacket said. They moved off to form the ambush at once and within an hour, without a single one of the saltmakers having become suspicious, the trap was set.

"It is on your head, Boone," Blue Jacket said. "They are your men. Are they going to live or die?"

Boone looked at him for a long moment and then spat to one side. "Reckon they'll live," he said.

Blue Jacket nodded, pleased, and told Boone to walk into the salt camp where the big iron kettles were bubbling and the fires sent blue smoke into the sky. He warned Boone to be casual and not say anything about the presence of the Shawnees until he was with the cluster of men. If there was the least suspicion that he was up to any tricks, the whole party, including himself, would be slain immediately.

Blue Jacket's maneuver moved precisely as he had planned it. As Boone approached them, the men clustered around him and in a moment they began sending startled glances toward the surrounding cover. Boone shook his head vigorously and spoke convincingly. After a few moments the guards carefully stepped apart a few feet and laid their rifles on the ground. At that, Blue Jacket gave the signal and the Shawnees closed in.

Inside of another hour the majority of their equipment was loaded on their packhorses and the white men themselves, their hands tied behind them and attached to one another with rawhide thongs, were being marched single file toward the distant Spay-lay-wi-theepi.

At the head of the party Blue Jacket smiled tightly, but inside he was exultant. What a coup! Not only the capture alive of twenty-seven saltmakers, their horses and equipment without a shot being fired, but the capture as well of the able frontiersman who had stood off Black Fish's assaults so well last year. The man called Boone.

Black Fish would be pleased indeed.

XV

Thursday, October 1, 1778

The feat of capturing Boone and his party was an exploit which made Blue Jacket something of a hero in the Shawnee tribe. Black Fish, who had become principal chief of the tribe following the murder of Cornstalk at Point Pleasant, was especially pleased and praised Blue Jacket highly in a council which included nearly a thousand warriors.

Since the British were warring with the Americans, a warm alliance had sprung up recently between the Shawnees and the army of King George III. In their western frontier post, Detroit, the British were paying well for scalps of Americans and even better for live captives. The decision was made to sell the saltmakers to them.

This was done, with the exception of Boone, whom Black Fish had come to admire so strongly that he adopted him into the tribe, giving him the name of Sheltowee — Big Turtle. But Boone, who at first seemed to adapt himself well to Indian life, insulted the tribe in general and Black Fish in particular by escaping several months after his capture.

The rest of the summer and autumn was an uncommonly eventful time in the Shawnee country. The nation had been preparing — with the aid of the British — to go against the Kentucky stations again, in retaliation for the death of Cornstalk. This was the main reason Boone had risked death to escape; to warn the settlements and get them ready for the coming attack.

Nearly five hundred Shawnees, plus a small force of British from Detroit led by Captain Isadore Chene, swarmed down against Boonesboro. But once again the sturdy little fort withstood the siege and after thirteen days the Shawnees and British had withdrawn. It had been an ill-fated expedition for them. Thirty-seven Shawnees had been killed and many of them wounded, but the Indians knew of only one Kentuckian who had definitely been killed.

They had returned to Chillicothe then and their depression was deepened by word that the split that had so long threatened to develop in the tribe was now under way. Well over half the tribe felt it was foolish to engage in another war with the whites and that the only sane course lay in moving west of the Mississippi River, beyond the reach of the white men.

The only bright spot of the whole time, in fact, had

been the capture of the young frontiersman named Simon Kenton, who was as widely known to the Shawnees and as much feared by them as Boone. This huge Virginian had long been a thorn in their sides and had slain many Indians over the years. At the council of Chillicothe, Kenton was sentenced to death at the stake. The execution was to take place at Wapatomica, the present hub of the Shawnee tribe.

From village to village Kenton had been marched northward, undergoing a severe gauntlet run at each. But at Mackachack,* principal village of the Maykujay Shawnees, Kenton leaped out of the gauntlet line and raced away with the whole village in hot pursuit. He outdistanced them all and had escape in his grasp when he ran right into Blue Jacket, who was approaching the village on horseback. Blue Jacket managed to cut him off and struck him with his tomahawk, fracturing the frontiersman's skull.

Believing they had lost him, the Maykujay Shawnees were overjoyed when Blue Jacket abruptly returned with his unconscious quarry. Once again Blue Jacket became a hero in the nation.

Moluntha, chief of the Maykujays and the oldest living Shawnee, paid honors to Blue Jacket, just as Black Fish had done. Because of his age, Moluntha was called King of the Shawnees and he was enormously influential in the tribe. The fact that he now took such pride and interest in Blue Jacket gave the twenty-five-year-old Shawnee even greater prestige in the tribe as a whole.

* Near the site of present West Liberty, Ohio.

Despite the excitement of these events, it was a comparatively calm incident which occurred in August that was most important to Blue Jacket. At his village on the night of the full moon in that month he had stood straight and proud in a line of twenty young men facing a similar line of young women standing fifteen feet away. The young Kispokotha subchief was excited over what was to come, but his face showed little expression.

Quite the opposite was true on the women's side. Their eyes danced with eagerness and they smiled boldly at the men, occasionally shaking themselves so that their long loose hair flared wildly and the contours of their bodies were outlined momentarily against the simple knee-length garments of soft buckskin. Now and then one or another would stamp her bare feet on the hard-packed earth.

Directly across from Blue Jacket stood the tall and beautiful visitor from the Maykujay Shawnees. For nearly a month now she had been visiting the parents of her Kispokotha mother here. Her eyes were large and dark and bold and her features very finely formed. Her high cheekbones gave way to smoothly tanned cheeks which framed a wide smiling mouth set with beautiful even white teeth.

This was Wabethe — the Swan — who was daughter of a warrior named Wabete — the Elk. Wabete was the younger brother of Moluntha. Blue Jacket and Wabethe had been unusually aware of each other's presence ever since she came here and the young man felt himself drawn to her as never before to another. That she felt this way, too, had become obvious on the night of the frolic dance ten days ago.

At that time a circle of men and women had formed around the fire, facing the circumference of the circle instead of the fire. Each man put his hands behind him and the woman who took her position behind him took his hands. Usually she held a cloth between them so their hands did not actually touch. But if the contact of hands was made without the cloth covering, it meant the woman had admiration and possibly love for the warrior.

Blue Jacket had seen Wabethe run lightly to take a place behind him and when the chant began and the forward shuffling movement started and he put his hands behind him, they were quickly grasped by hers and there was no cloth between them.

Tonight, at the far end of his own line of men, Blue Jacket heard the oldest man begin a queer chant. It went regularly up and down in tone and was monotonous, yet compelling. Over and over he chanted the words — *"Ya-ne-no-hoo-wa-no . . . ya-ne-no-hoo-wa-no."*

As he chanted, both lines began swaying and now men and women were inching toward one another. When they were about a foot apart, those in the line took up the chant themselves. Some merely repeated the same meaningless sounds of the chanter, but others sang words to the odd rhythm.

As the lines stopped, Wabethe suddenly put words to the chant. She leaned forward so that she was pressed against the broad chest of Blue Jacket and her face was very close to his. In tune with the chant she sang softly, *"Psai-wi ne-noth-tu"* — Great warrior.

They leaned the other way and it was Blue Jacket's turn. He pressed his own chest firmly against hers and replied in a husky voice, *"U-le-thi e-qui-wa"* — Beautiful woman.

Back and forth they swayed, each holding his hands clasped behind him, letting words and eyes and the touch of bodies relay subtle meanings.

"K-tch-o-ke-man," she murmured. Great chief.

"Ke-sath-wa a lag-wa," he replied. You are the sun and the stars.

"Oui-shi e-shi-que-chi." Your face is filled with strength.

"U-le-thi oui-thai-ah." Your hair is lovely.

"Oui-sha t'kar-chi." Muscular legs.

"U-le-thi ske she quih." Pretty eyes.

None of the dancers were saying the same thing except for the continued undertone of the chant, carried on by the old singer and a few of those in the lines. There was a murmur of highly personal whisperings as each of the dancers in turn, and in his or her own way, complimented his partner.

The couples, lost in themselves, heard nothing of what others said, not even those beside them in line. Only their own chanting was important to them and now the tempo of the dance picked up and they swayed back and forth faster and with deeper dips. Small beads of perspiration on Wabethe's upper lip and on Blue Jacket's forehead reflected the firelight in little sparkles.

Their words became even more personal now as in turn they commented upon each other's appearance and physical qualities. Then the tempo of the dance abruptly slowed and the dips became longer-lasting and a passion grew between the partners. For the first time their hands came into play, finding and holding one another.

This was the crucial time. If Blue Jacket remained silent now or told her *"Oui-sah meni-e-de-luh,"* — Good dance — they would part at the end of the chant and go their own ways. But now he leaned forward against her and his words were husky and urgent:

"Ni haw-ku-nah-qa."—You are my wife.

Wabethe smiled and placed her cheek against his and spoke softly in his ear. *"Ni wy-she an-a."* — And you are my husband.

In this manner did Blue Jacket and Wabethe become married to each other.

XVI

Never before had such a sense of grief, loss and despair touched the Shawnee nation. The hearts of her people were breaking and there was a pain beyond description in the eyes of all of them.

For so many years that it was difficult to remember exactly when they had started, the representatives of the five septs of the Shawnee tribe had been solemnly discussing what to do about the problem of the whites. At each such council it had become ever more clear that there would never be full agreement among them.

Those who advocated peace and the adoption of the white man's ways were more than ever strongly convinced that this was the only means by which the Shawnee nation could survive. Those who advocated war were equally certain that living under such conditions would be a life without honor, dignity or respect, to which death was preferable. And now, at last, a decision had been reached. Beyond any doubt, it was the most important event that had ever occurred in the tribe.

The Shawnee tribe split forever.

There were no tears, but there was a grief of unbelievable depth among them all. There was not an individual among those leaving this land forever who was not leaving behind a member of his family or a friend. And not one of those staying was not bidding farewell for the last time to parents or children or other kin, or to friends.

Moluntha and Black Fish, flanked by Black Hoof, Blue Jacket, Chiksika and Black Snake, stood quietly together by the side of the *msi-kah-mi-qui* and watched the loading of the packhorses. The French trader, Peter Loramie, shook hands with each and wished them well, promising he would return right after he had guided the great exodus to a new home across the Mississippi River.

At the head of the migrating septs were the chiefs Black Stump, Red Eagle, Ki-kusgow-lowa, Red Snake and Yellow Hawk. They were made up of nearly four thousand people, representing more than two-thirds of the Shawnee nation.

Only the aged and infirm among them rode horses. The rest walked and used their horses to transport their goods. It would take them nearly a month to reach their new land — a grant of twenty-five square miles on Sugar Creek near Cape Girardeau in the Missouri country. Peter Loramie had negotiated with Spanish officials on behalf of the Shawnees and had been heard sympathetically by the Baron de Carondelet, who authorized the grant.

And so now the assembled remaining chiefs watched in stony silence as the splitting of the Shawnee nation became reality. Leaving the Ohio country forever to seek peace were the majority of the Kispokothas, the Peckuwes and the Thawegilas, along with great numbers of the Chalahgawthas and many of the Maykujays. Remaining to fight until the last man of them should die, were for the most part just the broken remains of those last two septs.

Among those who had elected to remain behind and fight the whites was Black Snake, who had given up his leadership of the Kispokothas to Yellow Hawk in favor of remaining behind. He declared he would never make peace with the *Shemanese* and his second in command, Blue Jacket, had stood by him in this decision.

The result of the cleavage meant the abandonment of many of the Shawnee towns, particularly those along the Scioto River. Chillicothe itself, which had boasted a population of almost five thousand, now retained only about a hundred warriors. Black Snake decided to join himself to that village under the leadership of Black Fish and Black Hoof.

There were many of the Kispokothas remaining, however, who did not want to live with the Chalahgawthas and now these turned to Blue Jacket for leadership. Blue Jacket announced that they would form their own town near the Maykujay's principal village of Mackachack, which was the village of his wife, Wabethe.

It was not a large village and it was made up of a mixture of men and women from all five of the septs. It was located only a little way from Mackachack and it was called Blue Jacket's Town.* Blue Jacket was its chief.

Because his own sept was now virtually gone, Blue Jacket placed himself and his village under the authority of the old Shawnee he admired so much, Chief Moluntha, and the village became another Maykujay town.

The Shawnees had now, with this split, virtually abandoned eastern and central Ohio country and their remaining villages were in the western portion of that territory. They were located on the Little Miami River, the Mad River, the Stillwater River, Great Miami River, Auglaize River and Maumee River. But they were pitiful remnants of what was once a great and powerful nation.

Small though they were in numbers now, these remaining Shawnees became even more strongly welded together and more determined to fight to the death to protect this land they loved so much against the oncoming wave of white settlers. The war that had begun was far from over and it was their determination to show the whites that one Shawnee warrior was equal to any ten white men anywhere. It was a boast that would soon be put to the test.

But though these remaining Shawnees felt more closely drawn to one another, there was a great sadness in their hearts. The split of their nation had left behind

---

* Site of present Bellefontaine, Ohio.

an emptiness and loneliness the like of which had been unknown in their entire history.

For this, if for nothing else, Blue Jacket decided, the white men would pay a dear price for the land they were now preparing to steal.

XVII

Friday, October 15, 1779

Black Fish was dead!

The entire remaining Shawnee nation in the Ohio country was swept by an added sadness at the incident which took from them the most beloved chief they had ever had, and they swore swift vengeance. Of all who were sad, few were more grief-stricken than the chief's wards, Chiksika and Tecumseh. Blue Jacket came at once to be with them.

The death had been caused by a bullet wound and it was a long and painful way to die. Less than four months after the split of the tribe, an army of two hundred and sixty-four men, led by Colonel John Bowman, had crossed the Ohio River and ridden north to attack Chillicothe.

It was fortunate for the little army that this attack occurred after the Shawnee split. It was equally fortunate that at the time of Bowman's attack considerably more than half of Chillicothe's remaining warriors were attending a tribal council at Wapatomica. Had the first been true, Bowman's army would have been wiped out to the last man. Had the second been true, he would have been met by a hundred warriors instead of a total fighting force of thirty-five men and boys.

He was fortunate in these matters because even though his army outnumbered the defenders nearly eight to one, he suffered an awful loss, thanks to his inept leadership. Because of carelessness he lost the element of surprise and then, as they began to fight through the town, his men were overtaken by greed and began to pay more attention to looting the *wegiwas* of kettles, blankets, furs and silver ornaments than to fighting.

As a result, by the time forty of the *wegiwas* were burning, the Shawnee defenders, holed up in one strong *wegiwa*, had killed ten of Bowman's men with rifle fire, yet not a single Indian had even been injured.

Strangely, with the enemy in the palm of his hand, Bowman suddenly lost his courage and ordered a retreat. Overjoyed, the warriors managed to round up two dozen of their horses which the whites had been unable to catch and take with them. They set out in pursuit, caught up to the army and began to take shots at it from the rear. One by one they cut down men more interested in carrying away their plunder than in returning the fire.

The result was that more than thirty whites were killed before Captain James Harrod and two of his lieutenants, acting on their own, took command away from

Bowman and ordered a hundred men to throw down their loot and attack the small party shooting at them.

Rushed upon in this manner, the twenty-four warriors scattered and abandoned the harassment and returned to Chillicothe. They got there at about the time the rest of the town's warriors returned from Wapatomica to find their houses burned and their possessions gone. There had also been tragedy which resulted from the Indians' pursuit of the whites. Their third subchief, Red Pole, was dead. Black Fish lay in his *wegiwa* in great pain from a severe bullet wound. The ball had shattered his hip socket, shooting splinters of bone into the surrounding flesh.

In the chief's eyes was the sure knowledge of death, but there was also pride in his warriors for the way they had stood off the larger force. But the pride was soon replaced with great and growing pain. For three months he lingered, little by little slipping toward the brink. And finally, just before dawn three days ago, Black Fish had died.

The news had spread at once to all the Shawnees and from near and far they had come to witness the laying away of their great chief. For Blue Jacket and many of the others who came, it was the first they had seen of Chillicothe since Bowman's attack. Though the village had been rebuilt, it was only a shell of the great Shawnee center it had once been and they were shocked and angry. Instead of a thousand or more *wegiwas,* there were only a few hundred, and the ugly mounds of ash of those which had been burned still bore mute testimony to the attack by the *Shemanese.*

Inside the *msi-kah-mi-qui,* Black Fish was stretched

out on his back on a sort of low table. He had been washed and shaved and was now wrapped only in a fine new blanket. On the edge of the table and on the earth beneath and around him, there was a great collection of goods brought by his tribesmen, mostly belts and calicos and ribbons. Beside his body lay his four most prized possessions in life — his rifle, tomahawk, knife and pipe.

A great number of Indians were present and all of them wore loose clothing and their hair was unbraided. Many of the warriors had painted their faces in whorls of yellow and blue and vermilion. The men were smoking. As they entered the huge room they looked first upon the corpse of him who had been their leader, their old and beloved chief, their counselor in peace and war. Then they sat in silence on the floor wherever there was room. No one spoke and for hours they sat thus. Not a person present was without tears of grief in his eyes.

At last, toward evening, Chiksika and seven other warriors entered and gently slid four wide rawhide straps under the body. Each of the men gripped one end of the strap and together they lifted the body and carried it directly from the room to the burial ground two miles southwest of the town. No small child was allowed to accompany the procession lest he make some noise or cry during the solemn rite.

Immediately following the body walked the three daughters and two sons of Black Fish and the family of Pucksinwah, his charges. Behind them came the new principal chief of the Shawnees, Catahecassa — Black Hoof — and behind him came Moluntha, Black Beard, Black Snake and all the other chiefs and subchiefs, ac-

cording to rank. Walking beside Black Snake was Blue
Jacket.

Finally, some distance behind the chiefs, came first
the warriors of Chillicothe, then those of the other
Shawnee villages, all of whom were followed by their
squaws. Behind the squaws were the children between
ages eight and fifteen.

The grave was already dug. It was a long narrow
rectangle two feet across, seven feet long and three and a
half feet deep. At the bottom lay a screening, or
puncheon, of split and tied branches. Similar puncheons
were laid on edge along the two side walls of the grave.

With care, Black Fish's body was lowered until it lay
on its back on the bottom puncheon. Then the last clothing he had worn in health was placed atop his body. His
old moccasins were cut into strips and placed with the
other clothing. No weapon, food, or other memento was
put into the grave. A final puncheon was then placed
over the chief and the effect was something of a rectangular open-ended box within which the chief lay.

Then Black Hoof stepped to the head of the grave
and removed a cloth bundle from his belt. From the
throats of a thousand or more mourners there now came
the eerie rising and falling notes of the death chant, a
throbbing, melancholy sound filled with tenderness and
regret and deep despair.

Black Hoof opened the little bag and dipped his
fingers into it and then sprinkled some coarsely ground
material from it into the grave. This was *nilu-famu* —
sacred tobacco — a final sacrament.

Slowly around the grave Black Hoof moved as the

chant continued, sprinkling more of the grains at each step onto the platform below. When the bag was empty and he was back where he had begun, he dropped the empty bag onto the center of the top puncheon. Then he turned and headed directly back to the *msi-kah-mi-qui.* Still chanting, all but two men followed him.

Chiksika and Blue Jacket were the two who remained behind and only when the chant had become a faint sound in the distance did they set about scooping up the dirt in their cupped hands to fill the hole. It took them about half an hour to finish and then a smooth stone the size of a small pumpkin was placed at the foot of the grave and the pair, still without speaking, left the place and went straight to the nearby Little Miami River.

Here they stripped themselves and threw away their clothing. They entered the river and scrubbed down their bodies with handfuls of sand. Then each man thrust his fingers down his throat and forced himself to vomit. They moved upstream a short distance, drank until they could drink no more and once again forced themselves to vomit, thereby cleansing their bodies both inside and out. A short distance upstream on shore they found and put on the fresh loincloths awaiting them and then jogged side by side back to the village of Chillicothe.

When they entered the crowded *msi-kah-mi-qui,* quiet discussion was being held. Each person who cared to was contributing some special little memory of his own personal contact with the great chief. Outside, squaws were roasting a large quantity of game. As it was finished it was brought in and distributed to everyone present. In this way the ceremony continued far into the night. Not until the first gray shafts of dawn streaked the eastern sky did it end.

Black Fish had been greatly loved by his people. His death would be avenged.

XVIII

It was Black Snake and Blue Jacket who jointly led the Shawnees in the first blow struck to avenge the death of their chief. It was a harsh blow, too.

While they were still at Chillicothe, runners brought news of a fleet of canoes moving downstream on the Spay-lay-wi-theepi. At once an ambush was planned.

Though the Indians could not know it, this was the party of one William Rodgers, who fancied himself an empire builder. At Fort Randolph, he and his men had been warned against traveling farther downriver; had been told that of late an alarming number of attacks had been made on canoes by the Shawnees.

Rodgers almost laughed. What party of Shawnees would be foolhardy enough to attack fifteen canoes carrying seventy-five picked men armed with the newest and best rifles available? Why, if it came right down to it, Rodgers wouldn't be afraid to lead this very party of men on a direct invasion of the Shawnee strongholds. Fort Randolph's commander, he said, could better save his warnings and sympathy for any party of Indians they did meet.

An extremely self-confident man, Rodgers had labored long to build this large force. He planned to float directly to the mouth of the Ohio River and there, on the rich bottom lands where this river met the Mississippi, to establish almost overnight a settlement so well fortified that for the Indians to attack it would be suicide. This settlement would, in time, become a great western port city to be known as Rodgers — or so, at any rate, was Rodgers's belief.

As he anticipated, the flotilla skimmed past the so-called "most dangerous areas" of Three Islands and the mouth of the Scioto River without seeing more than a handful of Shawnees.* These had fled in apparent panic when well-aimed rifle bullets had buzzed their way. The party put ashore on the lowermost of the Three Islands, in fact, and camped here for two days as a sort of resting place before starting the second lap of the journey to the wide Mississippi. Precautions were taken and guards posted in the event an attack should occur but, as Rodgers had predicted, no attack came.

Now, far ahead where the Licking River joined the

* Three Islands was a stretch of river right next to present Manchester, Ohio. At the mouth of the Scioto River is the present city of Portsmouth, Ohio.

Ohio, Rodgers saw movement and quickly motioned his boatmen to put in to the Kentucky shore. Once on land he crept ahead a short distance to observe from cover. There, on a sand bar far out in the river, stood several Indians. One was Blue Jacket.

Even as Rodgers watched, a canoe paddled by three other Indians set off from the Kentucky shore to pick them up. Four more Shawnees squatted on the river's south bank, waiting. They appeared very innocently concerned with themselves and wholly unaware of Rodgers's approach. Rodgers licked his lips and grinned. Only ten Indians. What an opportunity to show the savages that his was not a force to be tampered with!

Immediately Rodgers ordered his boats made fast to shore and led all but a small guard detail in a wide sweep through the woods to encircle the savages. Apparently no one in the party was at all suspicious about the occasional bobwhite quail which whistled cheerily back and forth.

When Rodgers's line had taken position, hidden from view of the four Indians on shore, the canoe which had picked up the three off the sand bar was now almost back to the Kentucky shore. Rodgers held up his hand to signal a rush upon them, but the signal was never given. There was a roar as several hundred Indians leaped from hiding in a semicircle around the whites. A tremendous barrage of shots shattered the air, and even as Rodgers and the majority of his men fell, the Shawnee land party, led by Black Snake, dropped their rifles and fell upon the survivors with tomahawks and warclubs.

The ambush had been perfect. Except for the small

handful of men guarding the canoes, who fled through the woods at the firing, the entire party was wiped out. Rarely had so many fine scalps been taken in one fell swoop. Thus, in part, was the death of Chief Black Fish avenged.

XIX

The three years following the death of Black Fish were vicious ones along the Ohio River and in the Kentucky settlements. Although the dozens and scores of settlers coming down the Ohio River had increased to hundreds, even thousands, a good percentage were paying for it with their lives.

The Shawnees had no doubt now that their Can-tuc-kee lands were lost to them forever. Dozens of small settlements had sprung up and the larger ones, such as Harrodsburg, Stanford, Lexington and Danville, had now become substantial towns.

In June of 1780, Captain Henry Bird had come down from Detroit to lead his one hundred redcoats, seventy green-coated Canadian rangers and eleven hundred Indians against the settlements south of the Ohio River. For once the Indians had banded together for such a fight and the work was not all left up to the Shawnees. There were Delawares in this force, along with Potawatomies, Miamis and Wyandots, and even some Ottawas and Mingoes.

They had thrust deeply into Kentucky and destroyed Ruddell's and Martin's Stations, killing many settlers and escaping with a large amount of plunder. But in the retaliation which followed almost immediately it was the Shawnees who paid the worst price, since their villages were closest to the whites.

In August that year, George Rogers Clark led an army of a thousand Kentuckians and destroyed Chillicothe for the second time and even went as far north as the village called Piqua Town on the banks of the Mad River.* Here he met the Shawnees.

Since that first battle at Point Pleasant, Blue Jacket had stood out as one of the fiercest fighters on either side. His fame among the Indians, even those of other tribes, grew ever greater. But in this battle with Clark the Indians were badly outnumbered and outweaponed. Faulty flintlocks and simple tomahawks could do little against a superior force armed with new rifles and even artillery pieces. Before those cannons the Shawnees had been forced to flee. Both Chillicothe and Piqua Town were utterly destroyed and their surrounding cornfields burned. The whites had lost fourteen killed and thirteen

* Five miles west of the present site of Springfield, Ohio. Now the site of George Rogers Clark State Park.

wounded, but the Shawnees suffered losses three times this great.

The result was an extremely hard winter for the Shawnees, with food scarce and starvation a constant threat. To make up for their lack in food and clothing, they increased their attacks — mainly led by Blue Jacket — against the white boat traffic on the Spay-lay-wi-theepi. Dozens, scores, hundreds of boats were taken, their cargoes confiscated, their passengers slain. Without the goods these boats provided, along with a certain amount of British help, the Shawnees would not have made it through that winter.

When warmer weather came again, the attacks fell off and the Shawnees returned to the sites of Chillicothe, and Piqua Town, to rebuild their homes and replant their fields. Even though in October the Revolutionary War ended between the British and Americans in the east, here on this western frontier the friction continued, encouraged by the British at Detroit.

Again they sent a commander — Captain William Caldwell — to lead the Indians on another attack against the Kentucky settlements and in this one they had great success. First they took and destroyed Bryant's Station but, while the battle was in progress, some men who escaped carried word to Harrodsburg and a force of Kentuckians was quickly mounted to pursue and attack.

Aware that they were being chased, the Shawnees led the whites into a severe ambush at the Blue Licks. So successful was it that while hardly an Indian was killed or wounded, a total of seventy whites were killed. That number included some of the best officers then in Kentucky, such as Colonels Stephen Trigg and John Todd. Boone's son Israel was killed and Daniel himself wounded. It was a distinct victory for the Shawnees, but once again it led to an invasion by the army of George Rogers Clark.

The army crossed the river and headed north toward Chillicothe. When an easy ride away, they stopped for the night to prepare for the forthcoming battle. Clark wrote out his final battle orders for the morrow and posted them on a tree at the edge of the camp.

At first there was a good-sized crowd around the orders but it gradually dwindled. At twilight, only three men stood in front of it. The man in the middle read it aloud, slowly and laboriously. All three were dressed similarly in worn leathers, linsey-woolsey and moccasins. Each had a knife at his belt and one wore a tomahawk at his waist. All three wore fur hats made of raccoon skin.

The orders called for the men to pay the strictest attention to their duty the next day. Any prisoners taken were to be kept alive for questioning and possible later exchange for white prisoners. No soldier was to take any plunder for himself, but was to deliver it to the quartermaster where, after the battle, it would be divided.

When the one who had been reading aloud was finished, he spat a brown stream of tobacco juice to the ground and then grunted disgustedly.

"Clark's shore takin' all the fun out'a things, ain't he? Best part of going on these expeditions is killin' Injens an' takin' alls you kin git from 'em. First come, first served. Ain't that right, boys?"

The man to his left grunted an affirmative, but the

tall fellow on his left continued to stare silently at the general orders. The reader squinted at him and spoke again.

"Don't recollect ever I seed you afore. You new to Kentuck?"

The tall man nodded. "Got here just in time to come along. Came from my folk's place along Cherry River south and east of the Kanawha."

"That right? Me an' Jaybo here, we're from Pittsburgh. Never been down around your way. What's your name?"

The tall man shrugged. "Just call me Duke. Well, I'm going to eat now." He turned and sauntered off into the growing darkness.

Jaybo looked at his companion and grinned. "Them Virginny men talk funny, don't they, Mike?"

Mike nodded and spat again. "Yeah. An' they ain't too friendly, neither. Let's you an' me go eat, too, Jaybo."

Fifty yards away the man who had identified himself as Duke slipped through the undergrowth and silently crossed a creek in water just over his knees. On the other side he broke into a quiet run which continued until he reached a little clearing a quarter-mile away. There he ripped off the fur cap and shook his long black hair free and literally tore the linsey shirt from his back. He untied the horse waiting for him there and threaded his way through the dark woods for more than a mile before finally breaking into open prairie country and putting his horse into a canter.

Blue Jacket curled his lips. The very fact that he had spoken English left a bad taste in his mouth. He had been surprised at how difficult it had been for him to read Clark's orders. How many years now had it been since he had tried to read English? Not enough, he decided.

In a few hours he reached Chillicothe and spread the news; the *Shemanese* under Clark were coming again. And again there were not enough warriors here to face them. Retreat was the only answer, both from here and from Piqua Town. He would warn the others at Moluntha's Town and Mackachack, in his own town and Girty's Town, in Upper and Lower Piqua Towns and in Solomon's Town. The Shawnees, all of them, would gather at Wapatomica Town and there, with proper strength and weapons, meet the enemy.

And as Blue Jacket rode off, a fourteen-year-old boy moved into the shadows behind his *wegiwa* and clasped the piece of quartzite tied on a rawhide thong around his neck. It felt warm in his hand.

"Moneto," he whispered, "I call on you through this *Pa-waw-ka* to help us. Let us escape without harm except to our *wegiwas*, which can be built up again. Spare our elders and our women and children and keep our warriors strong. Let not the *Shemanese* destroy them. And most of all, Moneto, spare my brother Chiksika and my sister Tecumapese, and spare the members of our family. Guide and protect our battle leaders, Black Snake and Blue Jacket. I, Tecumseh, ask this of you through this *Pa-waw-ka*, which I earned here."

Then he went to where the others were packing to help them.

XX

Saturday, April 30, 1785

Clark's expedition had been victorious, but it was a shallow victory at best. All the Shawnee towns they had marched upon — Chillicothe, Piqua Town, Upper and Lower Piqua Towns — had been found deserted, with little real plunder left behind and no one to oppose them. These towns were destroyed, the crops burned and the army marched home again, satisfied that this time the destruction had been so complete that the towns would never be built up again.

The truth of the matter was that they had hardly returned to Kentucky before new *wegiwas* were being erected again over the ashes of the old. And now, once again the attacks against boat traffic on the Spay-lay-wi-theepi increased.

The Shawnees persisted in the belief that they would be able to hold the Ohio country against the whites, but it was a belief rapidly dying. Already white settlements were forming in the southeastern Ohio country along the river and now word had come through the British that Virginia was giving its soldiers bounty lands in the Ohio country as rewards for having fought well in the American Revolution. Connecticut, too, was claiming a vast section of the Ohio country bordering Lake Erie and calling it the Western Reserve. Settlers would soon be flocking in there as well.

To fight back against this encroachment and to continue to harass the whites at every turn, the Shawnees now looked more than ever to one man — Blue Jacket. This incredible chief seemed to lead a charmed life and his forays into the Kentucky country or against boats descending the river always seemed to meet with great success. Although Black Snake was still holding the title of war chief of the Shawnees, he was becoming old and slow and a little bit too cautious. In fact, it was Blue Jacket who was filling the post now.

On this morning at their *wegiwa* in Blue Jacket's Town, Blue Jacket and Wabethe lay side by side in their low bed and watched the first rays of sunlight begin to lighten the dim interior. Wabethe had awakened before dawn and was weeping when Blue Jacket awoke. Concerned, he had held her close to him and brought out the reason with a little coaxing.

"There is within me, my husband, no new little life which is a part of you. Not for a long long time has this been true and I fear I can bear you no more children." Her eyes were deep with longing.

Blue Jacket grinned, showing strong white teeth, and held her even closer. "Although it has been four years since the last one, my little Swan," he said slowly and softly, "do not think I will discard you because of it. No! I would keep you even should your hair become white and all your teeth fall away. What warrior would not keep such a woman as you? You have given me a son and two daughters. You are a part of my life and you always will be."

He leaned over and pressed his lips to her eyes in turn and then to her nose, but she pushed him gently back and shook her head. "You must get ready to leave now," she said. "The sun is up and you must not be late for the grand council meeting."

Nodding reluctantly, Blue Jacket stood up and stepped into his leggins and pulled over his feet the fine moccasins she had made for him. He was an impressive figure of a man. At thirty-one years of age he was still smoothly muscled and without an ounce of fat on his six-foot frame. His handsome face, framed by shoulder-length blue-black hair, was graven with lines of character befitting one of fifty years. There could be no doubt that he was a wise and strong man in the very prime of his life.

Carelessly but with smooth grace, he ducked into his soft doeskin pullover blouse and tugged it down over the broad chest. He drew his belt around him and thrust the pipe tomahawk into it, then scooped up his rifle from where it leaned against the wall. Automatically he checked the powder for dampness, as he always did upon rising. He tossed horn and pouch slings over his shoulders and then stooped for a moment beside the bed where Wabethe lay watching him proudly. He smiled and ran his hand gently through her hair, then touched his lips to her forehead.

"Go back to sleep, Swan," he said. "It is early yet." Then he was gone.

The sun was nearly straight up when he arrived at the massive *msi-kah-mi-qui* at Wapatomica Town. The sight of the huge building, as always, filled him with pleasure. Since the destruction of Chillicothe's big council house, this was the largest structure in the Shawnee nation. Over the years, how many wonderful and tragic things had he been witness to inside this heart of the Shawnee nation? And what was the reason that Molutha and Catahecassa had called this council? There were many more horses picketed than he had anticipated and his heart beat a little faster as he entered the door. Had another army been discovered crossing the river to march on them?

The room was well filled with warriors of the Chalahgawtha and Maykujay septs, but here and there were the few remaining representatives of the Kispoko-tha, Peckuwe and Thawegila septs. Chiksika and young Tecumseh were both there, as was the ugly old war chief he liked so well, She-me-ne-to — Black Snake.

In the center of the room by themselves sat the two most important chiefs of the Shawnee tribe, Black Hoof and Moluntha. Throughout the huge room were most of the other chiefs and subchiefs of the various villages.

Whatever the nature of this council, it was tribally important.

Blue Jacket took his place with the large group of warriors from his own town and filled his pipe. Others had already done so and a pleasant haze of blue-white smoke fogged the room as all present sat and puffed quietly. As the pipes were finished, their owners placed them in their laps or on the ground beside them. At last, when all the pipes had been smoked out and laid aside, Black Hoof arose and the faint murmur of voices stilled instantly.

"My children," he said, "we are come here for a most important matter. What will take place here today has never happened before and, I believe, will not again. It is a time of sadness and a time of rejoicing and I would ask our ancient King to tell you of it."

He reached down and took Moluntha's bony hand and gently helped him rise, then sat down himself. Moluntha slowly let his gaze sweep back and forth across the assemblage twice before speaking. He was becoming very frail these days and his long hair was pure white, his eyes nearly hidden in the deeply wrinkled face. Yet his voice, when he spoke, was still rich and strong and did not crack.

"My children, what Catahecassa has told you is true. This is a day both of sadness and rejoicing, but the rejoicing is the greater of the two and the sadness only aids in enriching the joy. I have seen one hundred summers. I am old and I grow weak. My eyes can no longer follow the flight of the pigeon nor my legs the trail of the deer. It is time for me to step aside as chief of the Maykujay sept and because of this there must be a sadness in my heart and in yours.

"It is my right, not only as descending chief but as eldest of all the Shawnees, to select the warrior who will be taking my place. He must be the bravest of the brave, the boldest of the bold. But he must be more than this. He must know when to fight and when to withdraw. He must be able and willing to think first of his people and, if necessary, to lay down his life for them. He must be proven in battle and in leadership and he must have the respect and admiration of all his fellow tribesmen. He must be wise and able to use his wisdom without pride; cruel, if circumstances demand it, but not make cruelty his master or his pleasure; kind, but not let kindness become weakness.

"The man I have chosen has all these abilities and more. Only the principal chief could overrule this decision of mine and Catahecassa has already told me he approves my choice. From this moment forward, the chief of the Maykujay Shawnees is the man to whom I now point —" he extended a bony arm "— he whose name is Weh-yah-pih-ehr-sehn-wah!"

And the heart of Blue Jacket, the white man turned Shawnee, nearly burst inside him with pride.

XXI

Tuesday, January 3, 1786

The small party of Shawnees led by Chief Blue Jacket
showed remarkable restraint in masking their anger and
disgust at the terms of the treaty they were now being
asked to sign at this new little fort. The fort was located
in the Ohio country just a short distance up the Great
Miami River from its mouth. Its very presence here was
an affront to the Indians.

And some of the statements in the treaty were almost
laughable, they were so contradictory. Yet both sides
pretended ignorance of their existence — the whites because they believed they were deluding "these ignorant
savages," and the Indians because objection at this time
could serve no other purpose than to endanger them.

The Shawnees were painfully aware that, although

this army colonel and his men treated them with a forced respect, each man in the company with the exception of the colonel carried a rifle. The twenty Shawnees were outnumbered nearly ten to one, so now was not the time to show the anger and the scorn they felt at these treaty proposals.

Colonel Richard Butler and his fellow commissioners, Captains Ephraim Lewis and Ebenezer Zane, had arrived here several weeks ago just as Fort Finney was nearing completion. The fort had been built on this bottom land with nervous speed under direction of its commander, Major Robert Finney.

The treaty being offered these Shawnees was simple and deceptive. Without ever mentioning the treaty held some time ago with the northern Indians, to which the Shawnees had not been invited and at which this very Shawnee land was allegedly sold, it reaffirmed the Ohio River as the border between Shawnees and whites. The only exceptions were the two forts and their sites — Fort Harmar, already built at the mouth of the Muskingum River, and this fort.

"The purpose of these forts," Colonel Butler said blandly, "is not one of invasion, but rather for your own protection. They are meant to turn back any whites who might try to settle on the Ohio side of the river. The treaty proclaims an everlasting friendship with the Shawnees. It is good to know that the differences of opinion between our peoples can now at last be put aside for all time."

The officers were surprised at the fluency with which Chief Blue Jacket spoke English and even more amazed when, with a distinct flourish, he signed the treaty with his Shawnee name, Weh-yah-pih-ehr-sehn-wah, and then added in parentheses, Chief Blue Jacket.

Colonel Butler looked at the double signature and then turned to Blue Jacket. He was obviously very curious. "Who," he asked, "taught you to read and write so well, Chief?"

Blue Jacket's answering smile was faint and cold. "My teachers were good," he said, "but I later learned to despise them."

After leaving the fort, the Shawnee band rode upstream nearly twenty miles before camping for the night. A light snow had commenced falling and the chief sat close to the fire beside Chiksika and Tecumseh. He spoke softly but his voice was bitter.

"I have never hated the whites as much as I hate them today," he said. "They are deceitful, treacherous, implacable enemies who should never be trusted in word or deed. They should be destroyed." He looked at the brothers and added, "They *will* be destroyed. Not now, because our party is too small and the weather too bad. But in the Green Moon we will return here in force, kill all these soldiers and burn this fort. Their presence here is an insult to our dignity and intelligence."

XXII

Sunday, April 9, 1786

The garrison had collected its gear and moved out of Fort Finney just in time. Standing now on high ground to the west of the swollen river with their company stretched out behind them, Major Finney and his adjutant, Captain David Zeigler, watched gloomily as the waters of the Great Miami River inundated the fort bearing the major's name. The flood had come quickly and now only the top of the blockhouse and the last eight inches of the wall pickets still showed above the swirling yellow waters.

With a disgusted grunt, Major Finney stood high in his stirrups and gave his men the command to march, leading them west toward the north side of the Ohio River just opposite the young settlement of Louisville.

Here he planned to build a new fort which would take the name of the abandoned one. But this one, he declared to Zeigler, would be built on high ground above flood level. No cruel hand of nature would destroy *this* one!

Not one of the nearly two hundred men in that column realized that the "cruel hand of nature" that had just destroyed the fort had also just saved their lives. At this very moment, less than thirty miles away, Chief Blue Jacket was leading a force of over five hundred Shawnees to storm the fortification and wipe out its garrison.

XXIII

Tuesday, October 31, 1786

Chief Blue Jacket didn't understand why it should be, but it seemed that no matter what Indians the *Shemanese* crossed over the Spay-lay-wi-theepi to attack, it was always the Shawnees who bore the brunt of the destruction. This time had been no exception.

In mid-September, Clark's army had crossed the river again, but this time it was known that he intended to angle swiftly to the northwest to attack the young confederation of five thousand Piankeshaws, Weas and Miami Indians on the headwaters of the Wabash River. The confederation had been established by the wise and fierce chief of the Miamis, Little Turtle.

As soon as they heard this, the Shawnees — every able-bodied warrior and chief — assembled and left to

join and aid the confederacy. But that's where things
went wrong. Clark's own spies told him that the Shawnees were moving to help the confederacy and so Clark
sent General Benjamin Logan back to Kentucky to raise
another army to attack and destroy the Shawnee towns
while he, Clark, continued with the primary mission.

Blue Jacket had thought that for once, with Clark
moving against Little Turtle's confederacy, the Shawnees would be out of the danger zone. And so what had
happened? Instead of fighting, the little confederacy had
listened to peace proposals from Clark's emissaries and
the Miami chief's allies had agreed and convinced the
reluctant war chief to do the same. This happened before the Shawnees arrived, and by the time Blue Jacket's
force got there, Clark's army was already moving down
the Wabash River toward the Spay-lay-wi-theepi and
their confederacy had scattered. There was nothing to
do but return home.

Then came the shock of getting back and finding that
General Logan's army had attacked and that thirteen of
the Shawnee villages had been reduced to ashes:
Mackachack, Moluntha's Town, Mingo Town, Wapatomica, Mamacomink, Kispoko, Puckshanoses, McKee's
Town, Waccachalla, Chillicote, Pecowick, Buckangehela's Town and Blue Jacket's Town.

The army of nearly eight hundred men had struck in
three wings and, with no one to oppose them but
women, old men and children, they had cut a great
swath through the Shawnee nation. Many Squaws had
been slain and some children.

Moluntha, seeing the helplessness of their situation,

had surrendered to Logan and was promised protection, but one officer had calmly walked up to the ancient unarmed chief and buried a tomahawk in his head, killing him instantly. Many of the squaws and children had been taken prisoner and might now be dead.

Among these were Blue Jacket's entire family.

A seething rage fell over the returned warriors. This anger made them want to turn immediately southward and retaliate on the Kentuckians, but common sense prevailed. If they did so, those women and children who had been taken prisoner would probably be executed.

Furthermore, new *wegiwas* must now be built to protect the remaining squaws and children from the forthcoming winter. And what little grain and vegetables that remained in isolated fields undiscovered by the whites must be harvested. Game had to be killed and brought in and the meat jerked. They needed to replenish stocks of salt, gunpowder, lead, clothing and furs and the best way to obtain these supplies was to capture the boats of the white men coming down the Spay-lay-wi-theepi.

Both Blue Jacket and Black Snake immediately led parties of warriors to the river and separated upon reaching it. Once again the watercourse became dotted with the wreckage of boats and floating debris — paddles and poles, the grotesque bloated bodies of cattle and the mutilated remains of whites. And north to the Shawnee villages flowed an almost constant stream of supplies. Among the loot that reached these villages were bundles of scalps. These were immediately relayed to Detroit to be exchanged for more supplies.

Now, as he leaned forward to cut away the bonds holding this white man to the tree, Blue Jacket wondered again why he was relenting in this manner. By rights, he should have tomahawked him in their first encounter. What had stayed the chief's hand was the remarkable resemblance of the settler to the father of Marmaduke Van Swearingen. And even when he questioned the man and learned that his name was John May and he was from the Limestone area of Kentucky now and Pennsylvania before that, yet the fact that this man *might* have been his own father bothered him.*

From the onset, May had been neither frightened nor defiant, accepting his capture by Blue Jacket as an unfortunate twist of fate. He did not want to die. But he did not beg for his life as so many did, and this pleased Blue Jacket because this was the way he believed his own father would have reacted. And so, for the first time since becoming a Shawnee, Blue Jacket allowed mercy to prevail in his decision.

"I will turn you loose," he said, "if you will promise to go back across the mountains to the east and stay there."

John May readily agreed and now he was free again, shoving his small canoe into the water of the river as Blue Jacket stood on shore with the settler's rifle. But before May was able to pull out of hearing, the Shawnee's voice came to him a final time.

* John May helped to found Limestone settlement which was built on land in part claimed by himself. Later the town which grew there was named after him and became present Maysville, Kentucky.

"Do not return to this country, white man. If I ever see you again, your blood will redden this stream. Remember that."

John May was not apt to forget.

XXIV

Saturday, March 10, 1787

Blue Jacket could not remember ever before having felt so nervous. It had taken many days to set up this day of prisoner exchange with the whites, and it was a wary and suspicious group of Kentuckians who met the Shawnee party under a truce flag here on the north bank of the Ohio River across from the mouth of Limestone Creek.*

On hand for the whites were half a hundred men led by Benjamin Logan. Blue Jacket was in charge of negotiations for the Indian side, but also on hand were chiefs Black Snake, Captain Billy, Me-ou-se-ka, Black Beard, Captain Wolf and more than sixty warriors.

* Site of present Aberdeen, Ohio.

The thought that today he would know whether or not his family was living caused the heart of Blue Jacket to pound heavily within him, but his face remained expressionless. The white prisoners had not yet been brought up from a place far back in the woods, nor had the Indian prisoners been brought across the river. They stood on the Kentucky shore in a cluster whose very silence spoke more of hope than any words they might have uttered.

Blue Jacket felt almost revolted at the declarations of friendship he had to give. Friendship! What could the treacherous whites know of this? The Kentuckians promised the same, but Blue Jacket told Black Snake in an undertone that they would see evidence of white treachery before this day was done. For their parts, the whites offered the same and promised to bury forever, from this day forward, the enmity between their peoples.

A well-hidden rage swept through Blue Jacket at the knowledge that this was an outright lie, but he said nothing. The prisoners on both sides were assembled and the exchanges made and it was a time filled with tears and cries of gladness and sorrow. Blue Jacket felt his heart leap when he saw Wabethe, followed by their son, Little Blue Jacket, and their two daughters, rush toward him. He embraced her briefly and touched each of the children on the head, but otherwise was expressionless.

There was a white girl of about sixteen who didn't know who she was or where she had been captured, and she looked at the white men assembled here and once or twice called out "Papa?" but fell silent when there was no answer. In another case a white mother was brought across the river from the Kentucky side to identify a girl of about nine. This woman had lost her child to the Shawnees when she was barely a toddler, but if this girl was she, there would be a triangular scar at her hairline where she had fallen once.

It was there! But though the mother screamed with joy, the daughter screamed in anguish, stretched out her arms to the squaw who had raised her as her own and cried out, *"Nik-yah! Nik-yah!"* — Mother! Mother! She begged the squaw not to give her up until at last the heartbroken Shawnee woman had to run into the woods with her hands over her ears and blinded by tears.

When the exchange of prisoners was completed without any form of ransom in money or goods being demanded by either side and an agreement made that all hostilities should end for the day, a huge barbecue was begun with two beef cattle and two elk.

The Indians were requested to stack their guns and, as the whites set the example, they did so, but kept knives and tomahawks in their belts. More of the whites came over the river, including many of the women, and quite a few of the people of both races relaxed a little and enjoyed themselves. Dancing was begun and the Shawnees smiled and nodded at the light-step reels. Then the whites watched in open-mouthed wonder the shuffling, circular feast dance performed by the Shawnees.

After an hour or so the festive air faded and the whites began moving to the boats and crossing to their own side of the river. The final three boats were going across when there was a fierce howling from the Shawnees. Gunfire sounded and little spurts of water erupted around the boats. The men in them were wise enough not to throw down their paddles and start shooting back, but to continue rowing for all they were worth until out of effective range.

Blue Jacket, his face once again set in surly lines, finally ordered the shooting to halt and the warriors to head back for their villages with the liberated prisoners. It was no satisfaction to him that his earlier prediction to Black Snake had come true. While the dancing and feasting had been going on, some of the white men had overpowered two Indians on guard and escaped across the river with fourteen Shawnee horses.

The peace had been a short one.

XXV

Thursday, April 24, 1788

Even though the bullet wound in his left side was not yet entirely healed and this raid into the Kentucky country had tired him more than he was willing to admit, Blue Jacket was pleased that he had come. None would have thought the worse of him had he elected to stay behind in his *wegiwa*. Even though the wound was healing well, with the drainage stopped and a scab well formed, it would not take much to break it loose again.

He had received the wound three weeks ago as he stood high on a rocky outcrop on the Spay-lay-wi-theepi, upstream from the mouth of the Scioto River. There he had watched a large flatboat drift downstream in the swift current toward the young river town of Maysville.

This was a good lookout point called Hanging Rock.

From its top a great vista of the Spay-lay-wi-theepi could be seen in both directions. Blue Jacket was nearly a half-mile from the boat and had even smiled at the little puffs of smoke which indicated the men had spotted him outlined against the sky and were firing at him. At such range and from a moving boat, they could not possibly expect to hit him. But then had come the tremendous blow in his side and the faint cheers from the men as he fell.

He had quickly plugged the wound with buzzard down always carried for such purpose and pulled himself onto his horse. He headed home, though he was somewhat foggy about most of the trip. He couldn't even remember falling from his horse just as he entered his village.

Wabethe had probed and found the bullet, removed it and dressed her husband's wound. For four days a great fever had ridden him, but her care had been good and he recovered quickly. When he learned of the projected raid to get horses from across the Spay-lay-wi-theepi, there was nothing else to do but take leadership of the party, despite Wabethe's protests.

She had bound him tightly about the middle and begged him neither to move suddenly nor stretch nor engage in running or jumping lest he tear open the wound and the red fire-in-the-flesh which he knew as infection should attack and kill him.

The night before they left she had presented him with an unusual but beautiful gift — a special hat she had labored over during nearly all the time he had been convalescing; a hat which was a talisman to keep him safe from all harm. Meticulously sewn together, it was a jet-black affair made of the feathers of crows over a skullcap type of base. A thin band of rawhide held it securely under his chin. Partially extended wings stuck out, one from each side, and tail feathers hung down from the rear. He accepted it gravely and told her he believed in its powers.

He had worn it all the way into the Kentucky country as well as during the time that fifteen of them had quietly stolen up in the dead of the night to Strode's Station. They had fed salt to the horses in the corral to quiet them and then had taken the thirty best ones and led them away without the whites even knowing they had been there.

About noon, when they reached the Spay-lay-wi-theepi near the mouth of Cabin Creek, five miles above Maysville, a cold misty rain had begun falling. Feeling reasonably secure from pursuit, he ordered that the horses be taken across and driven to their village. He would stay here to rest a few hours and then follow.

Unwilling to leave their chief alone in his weakened condition, however, two of the warriors returned after the horses had been swum across and built a fire in a relatively dry spot beneath a huge tree and sat around it with Blue Jacket. But the theft of the horses had been discovered within an hour and a dozen men, led by Jasper Hood and John McIntyre, had taken up the trail. They were experienced trackers and Indian fighters and the first that the three Shawnees knew of their approach was when shots rung out and one of the warriors slumped over dead.

Instantly Blue Jacket and his companion leaped to
their feet and ran in opposite directions, but the warrior
was cut down within a dozen steps. Jasper Hood, astride
his horse, galloped after Blue Jacket. As he overtook
him, he swung his rifle and the barrel caught the chief
alongside his head, stunning him. He managed to retain
his footing but, realizing the hopelessness now of further
attempting escape, surrendered. Within minutes Blue
Jacket's hand were tied securely behind him and he was
driven before the men, the rumpled crow-feather hat
still astride his head, though one wing was now
dangling.

They went first to Maysville and stayed at Boone's
cabin one night. The word of his capture spread and a
continuous procession of visitors came to gawk and jeer
at the feared Shawnee chief. His capture was something
to boast of and his presence something of a sideshow.
With their captives securely tethered, they also stopped
at Washington and Mayslick, Millersburg and Stockton's
Station. Finally, on the third night, they reached Strode's
Station again.

Though the exertions had ripped open his side
wound, Blue Jacket gave his captors no indication that
he was in any way in pain. Weary from their own exertions, the men tied the prisoner to a post in one of the
cabins, placed a guard over him and retired to their own
cabins to sleep before deciding what to do with him.
Less than an hour later, the guard had fallen asleep, too,
and Blue Jacket wasted no time. He knew he could not
free himself from the tight rawhide thongs which bound
both his wrists and ankles, but he had expanded his

chest as they bound him to the post and now these cords were loose.

Back and forth he leaned against the post and gradually it loosened in the earth until he was able to squat and, using the chest thongs for leverage, raise the post out of the ground. Very quietly then, so as not to awaken his guard, he lay outstretched on the ground with the post and managed to slip the thongs off the pointed end. When he regained his feet, these thongs fell loosely to the ground.

Now, ignoring the pain in his side, he began a series of short hops, each time landing silently on the balls of his feet and poising there a moment before hopping again. He had decided to make a great bound and land with his knees in the guard's middle should he begin to awaken; but the guard never stirred and his faint snoring helped drown out any sound made by Blue Jacket's light hopping.

The Shawnee chief raised the latch with his teeth and swung the door open with his shoulder, then hopped away into the darkness. The farther he got from the cabins, the greater his hops became and he did not stop until he was deep in the woods. At length, his lungs bursting and his injured side a mass of pain, he stopped and slumped to the ground.

He found that he could just reach the uppermost ankle binding with his teeth, though the straining made the pain in his side agonizing. It took him nearly a half-hour of alternately resting and chewing to gnaw through the cord, but at last it was done. He shook the cord away and, with immense relief, stretched his legs apart.

The wrist bindings, however, were very tight and not even rubbing them against a sharp rock had much more effect than to tear his own skin. Nor could he afford to spend any more time in this vicinity. He set off at an easy lope and before daylight reached the scattering of cabins which indicated Stockton's Station.

Crooning gently, he climbed the corral fence and stood poised there on the top rail until one of the milling horses came close enough and he leaped lightly astride its back. Startled, the horse partially reared for a moment, but Blue Jacket gripped tightly with his knees and continued his crooning chant. Gradually the horse settled down. With knee pressure he guided it to the gate and pushed off the two top bars with his foot. At an abrupt punch of his heels, the horse leaped the last low rail and Blue Jacket was on his way home.

It took him four days but he finally got there — hungry, thirsty, feverish and weak — and for the second time he collapsed and fell unconscious from a horse as he entered his village.

But he was back home alive and the lucky crow-feathered hat, considerably the worse for wear, was still upon his head.

XXVI

← ————————————— ◄

Saturday, October 30, 1790

► —————————————→

The last years had been ones of change. Though a few scattered families of the Shawnees still lived in the ruined town areas along the upper Mad and Great Miami rivers, the majority of the tribe had moved to the region of the Auglaize and Maumee rivers in the northwestern portion of the Ohio country. Here their villages were reasonably safe from white attack and yet they themselves could still continue to harass the whites in Kentucky and destroy boats coming down the Spay-lay-wi-theepi.

Relations with the whites had degenerated rather than improved and, though their war of the Revolution was over, the British in Detroit still encouraged the harassment and provided the Indians with food, weapons and gunpowder. And they still bought scalps.

But now the settlement of Ohio had begun in earnest. The newly appointed governor of the territory, Arthur St. Clair, had begun to partition the Ohio Territory into counties and new towns and forts were springing up. Three towns were now firmly established on the north bank of the Ohio River across from the mouth of the Licking River; North Bend, which was also called Symmes City, Losantiville and Columbia. St. Clair, however, did not like the name Losantiville and promptly had the town's name changed to Cincinnati. Here a very strong fort, impervious to Indian attack, had been built. It was named Fort Washington.

With its war with Britain more or less settled, the fledgling government of the United States now had time to consider at greater depth the problem of the western Indians. President George Washington authorized the sending of an army under General Josiah Harmar on a punitive campaign against the Shawnees on the Auglaize and Maumee rivers.

It was a strong army of fourteen hundred men equipped with good rifles, more than adequate supplies and even some cannon. But it was an army with a severe weakness — a commander who was both inept and cowardly. General Josiah Harmar was no longer the energetic and enterprising officer he had been during the Revolution.

The army began its march north from Fort Washington on October 7, but the Indians learned of its advance and prepared themselves. Once again the tribes combined into a loose confederacy made up of Shawnees, Delawares, Miamis, Potawatomies, Weas, Wyandots, Piankeshaws and a few Ottawas and Kickapoos. Two great warriors stood out as incomparable war chiefs and, unable to choose which of the two should have command, the Indians named them both as joint commanders. They were Little Turtle of the Miamis and Blue Jacket of the Shawnees.

By late October, when Harmar's army reached the junction of the St. Marys and St. Joseph rivers, where the Maumee River begins, the Indian force was ready and waiting. Harmar sent out two detachments of men to destroy Indian villages. One was successful but the other was itself destroyed to the last man by a howling mass of warriors.

Harmar panicked and ordered a full retreat, but his men were so incensed over this that they finally got him to stop some miles distant and send back a large detachment to find and bury the bodies of their comrades and perhaps engage the Indians.

This group, too, made the mistake of dividing itself into three wings and becoming separated. Once again the shrewd generalship of the two Indian commanders became evident when they decoyed one of the wings away and then swooped down and practically demolished the other two.

At this, Harmar fled south to Fort Washington, leaving one hundred and nine of his men dead on the battlefield.

It was one of the most shameful defeats in the young country's history; a defeat made even worse by the fact that, though the army was better armed and even had artillery, no more than a dozen Indians had been killed.

The fame of Blue Jacket and Little Turtle spread across the land.

XXVII

Although back again at the mouth of the Scioto River, Blue Jacket was still in an ugly mood as a result of the news he had heard before leaving his village. Two years ago, Chiksika and Tecumseh had journeyed south to the lands of the Cherokee and stayed with them for a while, helping them in their own battles against the encroaching whites. Tecumseh had gone away a boy but had returned a man. The stories of his incredible feats of daring and leadership and fierceness had preceded him. He had become a great warrior and some were already saying that one day he would lead the Shawnees to victory over the whites. But — and this was what had so deeply affected Blue Jacket — Chiksika had not returned. A bullet from the whites had caught him directly between the eyes, killing him instantly.

Blue Jacket's mood had not been improved by hearing from white captives he had taken from several boats on the Spay-lay-wi-theepi that a new army was being formed to come against the Indians. This army was to be led by none other than Governor Arthur St. Clair, and supposedly it would be a force against which no tribe, or confederacy, could stand. At this Blue Jacket smiled. How little the whites still knew of the fighting ability of the Indians.

He decided he would remain here for a few more days with his eighty or more warriors. They would take the five or six boats his scouts had reported were now coming downstream. Then he would return to the Maumee to report his findings to the other chiefs so that the confederacy could be reformed to again teach the white army a lesson.

As a runner dashed up with word that the first of the boats would be coming into sight in a moment, Blue Jacket motioned his men into cover. When all were hidden he turned to the two bedraggled white men sitting tied together on the shore.

"You know where we are hidden," he told them grimly as he cut away their bonds. "Your lives hang on what you do now. If you draw the boat successfully to shore, you will live. If you fail to convince the men to land, you will die. Immediately. It is that simple. Do not try to escape or warn them, or you will die along with them."

The men nodded, frightened, and got stiffly to their feet, rubbing their wrists where the rawhide had dug into the flesh. Blue Jacket watched them for a moment and then he too strode to the brush nearby and disappeared into it.

Within five minutes more a large canoe appeared containing thirteen men and two women. It moved out from around a bend into plain view. It was far out in the current but still much closer to the Kentucky side than to the Ohio shore. When it was four or five hundred yards distant, the two white men on shore began waving their arms and calling to the boat for help.

The craft came a little closer to shore, but not much. It was obvious that the occupants had heard how some of the Indians had learned to don white men's clothes and decoy boats ashore with memorized English words and phrases. The people in the boat had no intention of being so tricked. All fifteen people aboard suddenly had rifles at ready, including even the two women.

"We been prisoners of the Injens," one of the pair on shore shouted. "We got away. You gotta help us. Please, you gotta!"

The men in the bow shouted questions back at them. What were their names? When were they caught? Where? How did they get away? Where did they hail from? How could they prove they weren't Indians trying to decoy them to shore?

The men pleaded, answering all the questions. One identified himself as David Thomas, a frail and frightened-looking man; the other was a tough-appearing, bewhiskered individual who claimed his name was Peter Devine. As the two explained their capture, their escape, their origin and other matters, it became evident they could not possibly be Indians and the man in the bow of the canoe ordered the boat ashore. As it ground to a halt on the gravel, the leader jumped out and splashed ashore to tie a rope securely around a large chunk of driftwood.

The shots came just as he straightened — twenty or thirty of them at the same time. In that single instant, the lives of John May and his fourteen passengers were snuffed out. Instantly following the volley — at which Devine and Thomas had thrown themselves to the ground and cowered — Blue Jacket and his Maykujay and Kispokotha warriors emerged from the underbrush.

Blue Jacket stopped at May's body which was lying face down. As Devine and Thomas got to their feet, pale with fear, the Shawnee chief turned the body over with his foot. Yes, it was he — the same man he had captured near here four autumns ago; the man whose life he had spared because of his resemblance to the father of Marmaduke Van Swearingen; the man he had warned to leave this country and not return or he would be killed; the man who had promised to do so.

Blue Jacket smiled grimly as he drew out his knife and expertly scalped May.

At his command the other bodies were lifted out of the boat and dumped near May and also scalped. There were twenty-three rifles, kegs of gunpowder and much other plunder in the boat. Most of this, except for the guns, they ordered the two white captives to pile in a clearing in the woods out of sight of the river. The canoe and rifles, and then the bodies one by one, were also hidden in the brush.

They had finished just in time. Far upstream a warrior waved a signal that another boat was just about to come around the bend. The Indians themselves hid and once again Peter Devine and David Thomas took their places on the shore.

XXVIII

Friday, November 4, 1791

They were the greatest assemblage of chiefs ever to meet in the northwestern Ohio Territory. At the mouth of the Auglaize River where it emptied into the Maumee, which in turn rushed northeastward toward Lake Erie, almost three thousand Indians met in a grand council.

Though the tribes represented often had had squabbles among themselves in the past, now they put aside their differences and joined together to meet the greatest threat ever to face them. A great army had been formed under Governor General St. Clair at Fort Pitt. It had moved down the Spay-lay-wi-theepi, stopping to pick up more volunteers at Wheeling, Point Pleasant, Marietta and Maysville, as well as at its headquarters fort, Fort Washington at Cincinnati. Its prime purpose was to crush Indian resistance and build a string of forts from Cincinnati to the Maumee River to keep the Indians under control.

With artillery and horses and good weapons, along with the expectation of huge reinforcements and supplies to quickly follow, St. Clair had led his army out of Fort Washington. Twenty-three miles above Cincinnati, along the banks of the Great Miami River, St. Clair stopped to erect a new fort which he named Fort Hamilton.* On October 21, forty-four miles north of that site, he erected Fort Jefferson.† But then he began to have troubles.

His was an army of malcontents and during one night fully three hundred of them deserted. Fearful that they would meet and ransack the following supply train to obtain rations, St. Clair sent his best force, the First Regiment, in pursuit and then continued his march to the north with his remaining nine hundred and twenty men.

He marched his army straight into the worst defeat in the history of his country.

At their Auglaize River meeting, the Indians appealed to British representatives from Detroit to help them, not only with arms and ammunition, but with manpower. The British refused. They would provide arms, ammunition and powder, yes. They would even provide some of their better Indian agents, men such as Simon Girty and Alexander McKee and Matthew Elliott

* Site of present Hamilton, Ohio.
† The town there now is still named Fort Jefferson, Ohio.

— dressed in Indian garb, of course — to act as advisers, but they could not afford to become openly involved. The Americans would not need much of an excuse to march against Detroit and that important western fort must not fall to them.

And so it was up to these assembled chiefs to select their battle commanders and pledge their warriors and meet this white army with such power and spirit as had never been witnessed before. The first problem to be settled was who was to have command of the Indian forces. Again it came down to a draw between Blue Jacket and Little Turtle, and once again they were chosen as equal commanders. After all, had they not severely defeated Harmar's army last year?

Tarhe — the Crane — chief of the Wyandots, would be third in command and, following him, Chief Pipe of the Delawares. Waw-paw-waw-qua — White Loon — would lead the Weas and the few Mohawks. Thus it went, down the line through the Ottawas and Mingoes, the Piankeshaws and Eel River Miamis, the Potawatomies and Kaskaskias, the Kickapoos and Chippewas and Winnebagoes and others.

The Indian force had moved southward at once and when St. Clair encamped his army for the night of November 3 on the headwaters of the Wabash River, he was unaware that hardly more than a mile away, three thousand Indians were busily painting themselves and preparing their weapons for an attack in the morning.

Then came the dawn, Friday, November 4, a mean, gray morning of bitter cold. Low heavy clouds reflected ominous promise on the snow-covered landscape below.

St. Clair appeared in front of his assembled troops, raised his arms and spoke briefly.

"From intelligence delivered to me during the night," he said, "I am led to believe that we will be attacked by the Indians today. Perhaps very soon. All men will see to their weapons at once. Artillerymen will position and load the cannons. Emergency fortifications are to be erected beginning this moment."

But the time for such measures was past. With fearful shrieks, an unbelievable horde of Indians sprang from cover all around them and charged. On a dozen fronts or more, led by Chiefs Blue Jacket, Little Turtle, Pipe, Wingenund, Black Beard, Chiuxca, Buckangehela, Black Hoof, Tarhe, Black Snake, Sun, White Loon and others, the Indians struck terror into the hearts of the whites with their unexpected attack.

Scarcely firing a shot, the forward guard detachment of St. Clair's army abruptly panicked, threw down its rifles and ran for its life back toward the main encampment. Their panic was contagious and spread over the whole army, and in an instant the white force was in a state of deadly confusion.

A hot fire from the first line momentarily checked the main Indian advance under Blue Jacket and Little Turtle, but an immediate return of withering fire caused staggering army losses. St. Clair screamed for the artillery to fire, but for some reason only two of the cannon went off and neither did serious damage. At once Blue Jacket directed the greatest weight of Indian fire toward the artillery before they could collect themselves. In brief moments virtually all of the artillery men were down, dead or dying.

Never before had such a fierce battle been waged in the Northwest Territory. A din of fierce screams and cries filled the air and the snow-covered ground became a sea of red slush, stained with the blood of hundreds of men.

Colonel John Gibson of the artillery tried desperately to rally his few remaining men. "Fight them!" he shouted. "Fight them! Don't show fear. True Virginians never show fear. I'd rather die ten thousand deaths than let these savages take this field!" But he only died once. In that moment he caught a bullet in the spine and was killed.

More than any other Indian present, Blue Jacket seemed to be everywhere at once, rallying his own men, leading them into the hottest action entirely without fear or hesitation or seeming concern for his own welfare. He fought with fantastic energy and soldiers fell before him with regularity. Within the first half-hour, fourteen fresh scalps were wadded together in his pouch.

A regular army captain, Charles Van Swearingen, suddenly loomed and thrust a bayonet at him. The blade slit Blue Jacket's side and instinctively the chief wheeled and backhanded his tomahawk deep into the soldier's belly. The man fell upon his back and Blue Jacket pounced on him, grasped his hair in one hand and felt for his knife with the other. The soldier's eyes opened and then they widened, the fear turning to amazement as his gaze took in the features of the Indian chief. His gaze locked on the small white scar, like an inverted V, over the chief's right eyebrow — the scar that years ago, when they were boys, he had accidentally put there.

"Duke?" he whispered hoarsely. "It is Duke, isn't it? Don't you know me, Duke? . . . It's . . . it's your brother, Char . . . *Duke!*" His voice rose to a scream. "Duke, I'm Charley!"

He stiffened and then died and his body relaxed. Blue Jacket stared into his dead brother's face. It *was* Charley. A great roaring seemed to be sounding in his ears. No! He shook his head. No! He had no brothers but the Shawnees! With a flick of his knife he lifted the scalp and then leaped away to continue the assault, stuffing the hairpiece into his blouse and shrieking a cry that was more than mere battle lust, a cry which carried with it a deep inner pain.

The slaughter of soldiers was tremendous everywhere. Many of the soldiers, paralyzed with fright, simply stood in one spot trembling and crying until downed by bullet or tomahawk, knife or warclub. Nor was the slaughter limited to the military. The army had been followed, as was custom, by hundreds of camp followers. Some of them were wives but mostly they were loose women. Upon them, too, the Indians fell and the slaughter here was great. Within a span of an hour, over two hundred of them were killed.

For the first time St. Clair realized his army was doomed if it could not escape and he shouted orders for retreat. But it was not an orderly withdrawal. At the sound of the order the men cast aside their weapons and ran with all their strength to the rear. It was a complete and devastating rout.

All the way back to Fort Jefferson the army ran, walked or stumbled as fast as its remaining men could travel. The tattered, bleeding remnants of the army began arriving at the fort around dusk and there they met the most welcome sight imaginable — the return of the powerful First Regiment, which had been unsuccessful in its search for the deserters.

It was a solemn procession which slowly wove its way back to Fort Washington and Cincinnati. Their faces were gaunt and haunted, their eyes dazed and unseeing, their feet moving in a mechanical shuffle. There were no cheers and few tears; only a stunned and stricken silence as the residents watched the ragged remains of the worst military defeat in the history of the young United States.

The statistics alone spoke volumes: of the 52 officers in the battle, 39 had been killed and seven wounded; of the 868 regular soldiers and militiamen in the battle, 593 had been killed and 257 wounded; of the 255 camp followers, 220 had been killed and all the rest wounded. The final grim totals were almost beyond belief: Of the 920 soldiers who fought on that bloody field, only 24 men returned uninjured; 264 were wounded and 632 were killed. Taking into account the slaughtered camp followers, a final total of 852 whites had been slain.

What made it even worse was the fact that almost thirteen whites were killed to every Indian who died. Total loss for the Indian side was only sixty-six killed.

It was the greatest victory the Indians had ever had in a battle with the white men.

XXIX

Saturday, December 31, 1791

While the year ended on a more satisfactory note for the Indians in general, there was grief in a number of the Shawnee *wegiwas* as the brave warriors who had lost their lives in the victory over the *Shemanese* were mourned. Of the sixty-six Indians who had been killed, twenty had been Shawnees.

The most peculiar form of mourning was that done by Chief Blue Jacket. Though he was now being heralded as one of the greatest war chiefs in the entire history of the Shawnee tribe, for weeks after the battle he was silent and moody.

It was a depression which not even a most singular event could lift. That event occurred in the middle of the month when a deputation of British officers and soldiers marched to his village from Detroit. On behalf of the King of England, and with much pomp and ceremony, they heaped him with high praise, presented him with medals and appointed him to the rank of Brigadier General of the British Army. Never before had such an honor come to any member of the Shawnee tribe.

Yet even that failed to penetrate the gloom that had settled over Blue Jacket. A week after they were gone, with only a muttered phrase or two to Wabethe, Blue Jacket rode out of the village and was gone for nearly two weeks.

Alone the Shawnee chief traveled to the southeast until he reached Rattlesnake Creek. He traced its course to where it emptied into larger Paint Creek and then followed that watercourse thirty miles downstream to where it, in turn, emptied into the Scioto River. He crossed this larger river at the first fording place and then rode downstream along its east bank until he reached its mouth at the Spay-lay-wi-theepi. He saw boats filled with white emigrants going downstream to Manchester or Maysville or Cincinnati, but he avoided exposing himself and otherwise paid them little attention.

At length he tied his horse on a long tether at the base of a great limestone cliff overlooking the big river. Expertly, he climbed to that huge projecting shelf known as Hanging Rock. Along the way he gathered an armload of sticks and tinder and on the cold, bare surface of that ledge he built a small fire. Until it was burning well, he merely squatted and gazed into the flames. Then, from a pouch hanging around his neck by a rawhide thong, he removed the sand-colored scalp of his younger brother, Charley Van Swearingen.

With his knife he cut the hairpiece into small squares and one by one pitched them into the fire, watching the hair singe and burn and the skin portion curl and blacken into cinder on each one before tossing in another. While he did this, his voice rose and fell in the eerie, melancholy chant of the death song.

It took more than an hour to finish and when he was through, the fire had become low. With a little stick he scattered it and, as a plume of white smoked drifted upward in the cold air, Blue Jacket resheathed his knife. Then he stood up and, with his arms crossed over his chest, looked out over the broad dark Spay-lay-wi-theepi.

He let his gaze follow the river upstream until the water disappeared from view. For a long time he stood there and in his mind he was once again on that little creek bank in Virginia twenty years ago, bartering himself into Shawnee captivity for the life of his little brother. How frightened Charley had looked then and, except for his size, how remarkably little he had changed in appearance over the years that had passed.

When at last the cold air brought him out of his reverie, Blue Jacket turned away from the scene below. A single tear glistened on each cheek; the first tears he had shed in many years.

With his foot he scuffed into space the dust and ashes and remaining embers of the little fire. Then he began the slow descent to where his horse was tied.

He had loved Charley very much.

Tuesday, December 31, 1793

Another year had passed and the situation between whites and Indians had not changed. The United States Government now recognized, for perhaps the first time, that the Indians in the Northwest Territory were a force to be reckoned with.

President George Washington preferred, if possible, to deal with the problem peacefully. He dispatched messengers with peace overtures to all the principal chiefs, asking that they hold a grand council and discuss peace and a new treaty favorable to all. These overtures of the President came to nothing.

In some cases the Indians even refused to discuss possible negotiations and in those cases where they did hear out Washington's emissaries, they were scornful of

the proposals. What fools did the *Shemanese* think the
Indians were? How many times in the past had they
listened to such proposals? How many times had they
agreed, only to find themselves pushed farther back,
their land taken, their game destroyed?

Nor did it help the emissaries much when word came
to the Indians in June that the Can-tuc-kee lands were
no longer a part of Virginia; they had been made into a
state named Kentucky and were now a part of the
United States. As a result, the refusal to listen to the
peace proposals was sometimes extreme. Some of the
emissaries were slain.

Attacks on boats drifting the Spay-lay-wi-theepi
increased and onslaughts against scattered settlements
continued. Still, the government had hope for a peaceful
settlement. That hope was smashed late in the year. A
United States Army supply train of one hundred
mounted horsemen escorting a similar number of packhorses between Fort Jefferson and Fort Hamilton was
attacked by Indians under Blue Jacket and Little Turtle.

Fourteen soldiers were killed by the warriors. It was
the last important attack of the year and now the President knew the only solution lay in the use of force. He
named one of the country's most able military leaders,
General Anthony Wayne, to lead another campaign to
crush Indian resistance. Because of the dauntless way
the general led his men into battle, he had been nick-
named "Mad Anthony."

Wayne was a shrewd, resourceful leader and he had
no intention of making the mistakes Generals Harmar
and St. Clair had made. He formed his army and

marched it in early winter to Fort Jefferson, but found the fort small and ill-fitted. So five miles north he ordered the construction of a new fort, which he named Fort Greenville. Here the army would winter and, as soon as the weather became better, the campaign would begin in earnest.

Wayne also sent a detachment to build another fort on the site of St. Clair's defeat, this fort to be named Fort Recovery.* The detachment sent to do the job arrived there on Christmas Day and met a horrible sight. Skulls were strewn everywhere and before they could lie down in the tents they had pitched on the old battlefield, the scattered bones had to be scraped together and carried outside. The next day holes were dug and the bones remaining above the ground were buried; this included no less than six hundred of the skulls.

Wayne's preparations for war did not keep him from continuing his efforts at establishing peace with the Indians. But, as with George Washington's efforts, such messages were received with scorn and in some cases the messengers did not return.

Both Indians and British remained worried about Wayne's preparations for war. Another great council of the confederated tribes was held and there was no doubt that the Indians were, on the whole, looking forward to the next battle. After all, had they not defeated General Harmar's army? Had they not virtually annihilated St. Clair's army? Why would they not be able to do so with Wayne as well, especially if Little Turtle and Blue Jacket should again lead them?

* The town bears this same name today.

But for once Little Turtle was hesitant. He did not think it wise to oppose Wayne and urged that the confederacy try to reach some peaceful compromise with the whites. The Indians were shocked to hear this from the great war chief of the Miami tribe and several of the other chiefs accused Little Turtle of cowardice and of becoming too old. Surprisingly, he did not take great offense at this. Instead, he raised his hands and spoke solemnly:

"We have beaten the enemy twice under separate commanders. We cannot expect the same good fortune always. The Americans are now led by a chief who never sleeps. The night and the day are alike to him and during all the time that he has been marching on our villages, notwithstanding the watchfulness of our young men, we have never been able to surprise him. There is something whispers to me that it would be prudent to listen to his offers of peace."

The discussions continued but it was obvious that now, although Little Turtle bowed to the will of the council and said he would fight if that was their desire, the chief of the Miami tribe would not be the commander of the Indians for this forthcoming battle. The Indians needed a man proved worthy in warfare and leadership; a man with strength and cunning and ferocity; a man who had the respect not only of his own tribe, but all the other tribes. And they had just such a man.

Unanimously, Blue Jacket — Brigadier General and war chief of the Shawnees, as well as chief of the Maykujay sept — was appointed as commander-in-chief of the Indian forces.

Honored, Blue Jacket accepted, but his heart was not

in it. Deep inside, he believed that Little Turtle was right this time. And since that day he had slain his own brother in battle, something had not been quite the same with him. A certain drive and vitality had gone.

It was something he would never again feel.

XXXI

Friday, August 7, 1795

The confederation of Indian tribes should have heeded the words of Chief Little Turtle.

More than ever the British alarm over Wayne's presence and plans grew. They believed that it was Mad Anthony's plan, if given the least cause, to take Detroit itself. And so, in April of 1794, Lieutenant Governor John Simcoe of British Canada left Detroit accompanied by an expert staff of Indian agents, military officers and engineers.

They sailed down the Detroit River and across the western end of Lake Erie, then up the Maumee River to the foot of a large rapids.* There, on the north bank of the river near the ruins of the old British fort abandoned

* Near the site of present Waterville, Ohio.

at the close of the Revolution — and where Indian agent Alexander McKee currently maintained a trading post — Simcoe ordered a fort built. This was in strict violation of the British-American treaty. He named it Fort Miami after the Maumee River, which was also known as the Miami-of-the-Lake. Almost immediately there was an influx of Indians to the King's Store in the fort to receive free arms and ammunition for the coming battle.

In June, a white renegade named Harry May deserted the Indians and brought word to General Wayne of a force of Indians being led by Blue Jacket to destroy Fort Recovery. Wayne sent a detachment of reinforcements to the fort under Major McMahon. In the brief battle there, the major was killed. But Mad Anthony had built his fort well and the walls were not breached. After two days of fighting, Blue Jacket ordered his men to pick up the dead warriors and the Indian force left as quickly as it had come.

Now it was Wayne's turn to take up the offensive. He led his army north to the Auglaize River and followed that stream down to where it joined the Maumee. Here he built another fort in eight days and it was so strong a fort that the general looked at it and said:

"I defy the English, Indians and all the devils in Hell to take it!"

General Charles Scott, standing at Wayne's side, remarked, "Then call it Fort Defiance." And Wayne did so. *

Harry May, the renegade, was recaptured by the Shawnees and taken to a spot within sight of Fort

---

* Site of present Defiance, Ohio.

Miami. For his treachery, death was the only reward. He was tied to a tree and a mark painted on his bare chest. Fifty Indians with flintlocks fanned out in a semicircle and at a command from Blue Jacket, all fired simultaneously. No more damage could have been done to May had he been struck full in the breast with an eight-pound cannonball.

Wayne continued his march down the Maumee and at the Rapids, in an area where wind-downed trees cluttered the ground, the battle was begun — a battle afterwards known as the Battle of Fallen Timbers. It was a severe contest, but it soon became apparent that the Indians had more than met their match. The entire Indian line collapsed and the warriors began to flee in disorder, despite Blue Jacket's rallying cries. They left behind a hundred dead Indians.

The British garrison in Fort Miami watched the battle in silence. The gate was closed and locked and they offered no assistance to the Indians, even when they came to the walls and demanded it. With this failure of promised British aid, the Indians lost heart and scattered and the battle was over.

For weeks afterwards Wayne moved about the countryside up and down the length of the Maumee, burning Indian villages and grainfields. Then he marched his army back to Fort Greenville, arriving there on November 2. It was a long-awaited victory.

Now it was winter which became a greater foe to the Indians. They had camped at the mouth of Swan Creek* and were hard put to stay alive. With their fields, goods

* Site of present Toledo, Ohio.

and homes destroyed, they had become largely depen-
dent upon the British, but now the British didn't help
them nearly enough.

The defeat and famine were enough to discourage
anyone, but even then the Indians might have fought on
if something hadn't happened which they considered a
supernatural omen. To their way of thinking, it was such
a portent of evil to come that they resigned themselves
to surrendering to the Americans and asking them for
more help than they were getting from the British.

The incident was indeed a strange one. Of all the
white men known by the confederated Indians, none had
so much influence among them or received as much
respect from them as Colonel Alexander McKee. It was
he, more than anyone, who had always heretofore made
certain that the British lived up to their promises to
provide food, firearms and various goods to them. And
when these items did not arrive in time, it was McKee
who single-handedly stormed Detroit and demanded the
promises be met.

The agent was a fierce fighter as well and few major
battles had been fought in which he was not present and
at all times in the thick of things. Yet never once was he
wounded in any way, and this made the Indians believe
that he was under the special protection of the Great
Spirit. There was further belief that the Great Spirit
manifested Himself in McKee's pet deer, which followed
him about with the devotion of a dog.

And then came that morning at home, while he was
dressing, when something seemed to come over the animal. As McKee bent over to thrust his leg into his

trousers, the fully antlered buck charged and caught him squarely in the rear.

It might have been a funny thing, except for the results. The prongs of the antlers plunged deeply into McKee's flesh, and one of them entered his thigh and punctured the huge femoral artery. McKee, who had been sent sprawling, raised himself to a sitting position and with dazed eyes watched his lifeblood drain out to become a wide scarlet puddle on the floor. Within minutes he was dead.

And so, with this seemingly supernatural occurrence to add to their fear and depression, their hunger and need, representatives of the tribes came to Fort Greenville and asked Wayne for peace. The general accepted the offers tentatively and an agreement was made for all the principal chiefs to meet at the fort in the summer to conclude a permanent peace treaty.

They came. The Delawares, under chiefs Buckangehela, Teteboxti and Peke-tele-mund, made up the largest single Indian group, numbering 381 individuals. There were also 240 Potawatomies under Chiefs New Corn, Asimethe and Sun, and 180 Wyandots under Chief Tarhe. Black Hoof, Black Snake and Blue Jacket came with a party of 143 Shawnees and Little Turtle arrived solemnly leading 73 Miamis, including 22 Eel River Miamis under Chief Legris. Forty-six Chippewas attended under chiefs Massas and Bad Bird, while the 45 Ottawas were represented by Chief Augooshaway. A dozen Weas and Piankeshaws came under the leadership of Chief Reyntwoco and 10 Kickapoos and Kaskaskias arrived under Chief Keeahah.

In all, there were twelve tribes represented, totaling 1,130 men. The negotiations were begun at once. The terms dictated by Wayne made none of the Indians happy.

According to the treaty, the Indians would be permitted to retain the privilege of hunting and fishing throughout the Ohio country, all the way to the Ohio River, but not across it. The new dividing line between Indian and white territories however, was to be a line which gave the whites twenty-five thousand square miles of Ohio Territory; which was more than half of the whole Ohio country. In addition, the United States would claim sixteen tracts *within* the Indian territory, each about six miles square, for government reservations and the building of forts.

For giving up the Ohio land now claimed by the United States, the Indians were to receive goods to the value of $1,666 for each of the twelve tribes represented here, plus an annual allowance to each of the tribes of $825 in goods.

This was not an easy treaty to agree on. Chief after chief spoke at great length and at first there were strong opponents. Among them were Blue Jacket, Little Turtle and Black Snake. But these three were well aware that they had little choice. Better, perhaps, for all the chiefs to sign this document and make the best of it, adhering closely to its limitations and seeing to it that the whites did the same, thus salvaging some of their land as well as some of their pride. To continue hostilities would be to lose everything. None of them had any doubt of this and they were tired of war and longed for peace.

On August 3, all of the chiefs representing the tribes signed the Treaty of Greenville, as did General Wayne. And today, August 7, the general gave his farewell address to the Indians.

"I now fervently pray to the Great Spirit," he said, "that the peace now established may be permanent and that it now holds us together in the bonds of friendship until time shall be no more. I also pray that the Great Spirit above may enlighten your minds and open your eyes to your true happiness, that your children may learn to cultivate the earth and enjoy the fruits of peace and industry."

Thus, officially and at long last, ended the Indian wars in the Northwest Territory.

So everyone claimed, at least.

XXXII

Tuesday, June 26, 1810

The vital spark that had gone out of Blue Jacket when he had slain his own brother, Charley, had never returned. And with peace over the land, he retired to his own village where he had spent these past fifteen years with his wife, Wabethe. All three of their children had now married and gone their own ways.

For the Shawnees, Blue Jacket was happy at the peace and the fact that an Indian might now meet a white man on the trail without fear of instant conflict and possible death. But, equally, he was sorry for them — and for all Indians — for he knew now with deathless certainty that the words of Pucksinwah almost forty years ago were true: there could never be an equitable, lasting peace between Indians and whites.

It was obvious that sometime in the years ahead another showdown must come between them. Once again the whites were encroaching in the Indian territories. But Blue Jacket knew this time that if a showdown did come, the Indian forces would not be led by himself.

Blue Jacket was dying.

His fifty-six-year-old body wracked with the dread disease known as cholera, he lay wasting away in his *wegiwa*. Beside the low bed, Wabethe sat on the floor holding his hot, dry hand. For two days he had been out of his head with delirium and during all this time she had sat thus, watching him, tending him, moistening his constantly dry mouth. At last she had fallen into an exhausted sleep and it was then, as death approached, that Blue Jacket had a moment of clarity.

He looked over at Wabethe, still holding his hand, her head leaning against him as she slept, and he smiled. How good a wife she had been, and how much he still loved her.

He did not awaken her, but let his mind drift lazily over the many things that had happened during his life It had been a good life and he had no wish that he might have lived it in another way, except that perhaps his efforts on behalf of his people, the Shawnees, might have borne more fruit.

Perhaps yet they might. Perhaps in Tecumseh the Shawnees might still regain that which they had lost. He remembered clearly the visit he had paid to the son of Pucksinwah shortly after the Treaty of Greenville had been concluded. Although Tecumseh had been invited to attend these negotiations, he had refused.

The young chief had listened to Blue Jacket tell what had occurred at Fort Greenville and then he had shaken his head sadly. By the terms of that treaty, the very land upon which Tecumseh's village stood belonged to the whites and he and his followers would have to vacate themselves.

"I do not hold with such a treaty," he had told Blue Jacket. "Such agreements with whites have always been and will always be wholly worthless. My people and I will remain here until our corn is harvested and our winter hunting completed. Only then, when melting snows swell the rivers, will we move away into what the whites still consider Indian lands."

Tecumseh had paused a long time and when he had finally spoken again, his voice was low and his words were filled with a great bitterness.

"My heart," he said, "is a stone: heavy with sadness for my people and my race; cold with the knowledge that no treaty will keep the whites out of our lands, no matter where we move; hard with the determination to resist as long as I live and breathe.

"Now we are weak," he continued, "and many of our people are afraid. But hear me: a single twig breaks easily, but the bundle of twigs is strong. Someday I will journey in all directions and one by one I will embrace our brother tribes and draw them into a bundle. Then, when we are strong and united, then will we, together, win our country back from the whites!"

Again Blue Jacket smiled as he remembered the

intensity with which Tecumseh had spoken. He had slowly nodded his head and replied, "Yes, I think perhaps you will."

And now, looking back over what had happened in these years, Blue Jacket thought again that perhaps Tecumseh would do just as he had promised he would. He had visited the tribes to north and south, to east and west and he had drawn them together in the greatest confederation ever known among Indian nations. The influence he bore now among them was certainly greater than any single Indian had ever held before.

War was coming soon, very soon. Of that, Blue Jacket had no doubt. And possibly, just possibly, Tecumseh was the man who would lead the Indians to complete victory.

Blue Jacket sighed faintly and wished that he might have been able to take part in the desperate struggle which lay ahead. He looked over again at Wabethe and his mouth corners twitched in just the faintest trace of a smile.

And then he closed his eyes and died.